The Mysterious Voyage
of
Captain Kidd

The Mysterious Voyage of *Captain Kidd*

A.B.C. Whipple

illustrated by H.B. Vestal

Purple House Press
Cynthiana, Kentucky

This one is for
Abigail

Grateful acknowledgment is due to Houghton Mifflin Company for permission to adapt the map of Kidd's voyage by Samuel H. Bryant from *No Man Knows My Grave* by Alexander Winston.

Published by
Purple House Press
PO Box 787
Cynthiana, Kentucky 41031

Classic Books for Kids and Young Adults
purplehousepress.com

Copyright © 1970 by A.B.C. Whipple
All rights reserved.
Value of Captain Kidd's cargo adjusted for inflation from 1970 to 2020.
CIP data is available upon request. LCCN 2021029269

ISBN 9781948959544 Hardcover
ISBN 9781948959551 Paperback

CONTENTS

1.	Before the Silver Oar	3
2.	A Prosperous Merchant	5
3.	The Mysterious Syndicate	15
4.	*Adventure Galley* Sets Sail	28
5.	East to Madagascar	37
6.	Action at Sea	50
7.	A Mutinous Crew	63
8.	The Great Prize	73
9.	Buried Treasure	89
10.	Trial and Treachery	103
11.	Pirate or Privateer?	118
	MAP: Kidd's Voyage	38
	AUTHOR'S NOTE	129
	PUBLISHER'S NOTE	130
	INDEX	131
	ABOUT THE AUTHOR AND ILLUSTRATOR	137

The Mysterious Voyage
of
Captain Kidd

The Mysterious Voyage
of
Captain Kidd

1

Before the Silver Oar

"William Kidd, hold up thy hand."

He was a small man. As he stood in the prisoner's dock, his clothes seemed to hang on him. His face was gray. His mustache and hair were unkempt. His figure was stooped, and he seemed almost too weak to raise his right arm.

He had been in London's Newgate Jail for more than a year. For the last two days he had tried to defend his name, his honor, and his life in the Admiralty Court. Now he was exhausted and beaten. He faced the six black-robed Admiralty judges and awaited the sentence he knew was to come.

Their faces, under their white wigs, had no expression. In front of them lay the symbol of their authority—the Silver Oar of the Admiralty Court. It was also the symbol of the law of the sea. He had been convicted of breaking that law. So the Silver Oar, Kidd knew, would be carried before him when he was taken to the gallows.

The voice of the chief judge was already pronouncing sentence: "…there you will be hanged by your neck until dead.

"And the Lord have mercy on your soul."

They say that a man's whole life passes before his eyes when he knows he is going to die. But as Captain William Kidd was led out of the Admiralty Court to Newgate Jail, he may have thought back for only six years. It had all happened in six swift years. Six years ago Captain Kidd had been a prosperous merchant in New York City, with a wife and a daughter and a legion of friends. Now he was in Newgate Jail in London, convicted of piracy and murder, and sentenced to be hanged by his neck until dead. How, Captain William Kidd must have wondered, could all this have happened to him in only six years?

This book is about how it happened.

1

BEFORE THE SILVER OAR

"William Kidd, hold up thy hand."

He was a small man. As he stood in the prisoner's dock, his clothes seemed to hang on him. His face was gray. His mustache and hair were unkempt. His figure was stooped, and he seemed almost too weak to raise his right arm.

He had been in London's Newgate Jail for more than a year. For the last two days he had tried to defend his name, his honor, and his life in the Admiralty Court. Now he was exhausted and beaten. He faced the six black-robed Admiralty judges and awaited the sentence he knew was to come.

Their faces, under their white wigs, had no expression. In front of them lay the symbol of their authority—the Silver Oar of the Admiralty Court. It was also the symbol of the law of the sea. He had been convicted of breaking that law. So the Silver Oar, Kidd knew, would be carried before him when he was taken to the gallows.

The voice of the chief judge was already pronouncing sentence: "…there you will be hanged by your neck until dead.

"And the Lord have mercy on your soul."

They say that a man's whole life passes before his eyes when he knows he is going to die. But as Captain William Kidd was led out of the Admiralty Court to Newgate Jail, he may have thought back for only six years. It had all happened in six swift years. Six years ago Captain Kidd had been a prosperous merchant in New York City, with a wife and a daughter and a legion of friends. Now he was in Newgate Jail in London, convicted of piracy and murder, and sentenced to be hanged by his neck until dead. How, Captain William Kidd must have wondered, could all this have happened to him in only six years?

This book is about how it happened.

A Prosperous Merchant

In 1695, over three centuries ago, New York was not even a city. It was a port town with about five thousand people, fewer than the number of students in most medium-sized colleges today. New York was small, but so were the rest of the settlements in the New World. And of all those settlements, New York was the liveliest. Boston was more important. Philadelphia had more prestige. Virginia was older. But New York was where the action was.

New York was full of travelers from all over the world. More than a dozen different languages could be heard along the wharves. There were Dutchmen

in duffels and woolen caps. There were Englishmen in bell-bottomed trousers. There were Spaniards with cutlasses hanging from their wide leather belts. There were West Indians in striped smocks. And there were swaggering sailors of fortune, wearing a single gold earring and sometimes carrying a parrot on a broad shoulder. The sailors' hangouts along Dock Street and Great Queen Street were filled with a colorful gathering from all over the globe.

These were the men who provided the crews for the countless ships that came and went from the port town of New York. The men who owned and captained these ships lived only a block or two away, in their mansions on the tree-lined streets overlooking the waterfront. And one of the most substantial of these homes was that of William Kidd.

It was an impressive brick house with a view of the East River, just north of the Great Dock, the center of activity for New York harbor. From his windows Captain Kidd could see every ship that came into port. And it was only a short walk to the business center of New York, with the Customs House, the warehouses, and the lines of merchant shippers' offices.

Captain Kidd owned other pieces of land, on Pearl Street, on Water Street, on Pine Street, and on Wall Street. The Wall Street house had once belonged to a wealthy New York widow, Mrs. Sarah Oort. When

William Kidd had tried to buy it from her, she had refused to sell it. Evidently Sarah Oort had a better idea, because three years later she became Mrs. William Kidd. Now they had a baby daughter. Her name was Elizabeth.

William Kidd was one of the pillars of the New York community. He had come to the American colonies from Scotland, after shipping out as a young man before the mast. By 1695 he had risen to captain and even had a small fleet of his own. Most of his business was in the West Indies, and Captain Kidd had commanded his own trading vessels on voyages to the islands. Those were the days when the merchants of New York, Philadelphia, and Boston sent their ships down to the Caribbean with flour, timber, and fish, exchanging them for sugar, rum, and molasses from the islands.

It was a popular and profitable business. William Kidd and the other merchant skippers of New York made money and lived elegantly in their big houses, surrounded by luxuries they could afford to bring in from all over the world. In New York the first business was making money, and the second business was enjoying it. New Yorkers raced horses, gambled, played cards, and concentrated on having a good time—unlike those Bostonians and Philadelphians. And New Yorkers, like the people in any colonial center, did their best to imitate the elegant life of London. But then, from London, came a major threat to the good times of New York.

Those New York merchant skippers had begun to cut into the business of the merchants of London, especially their business in the West Indies. The American colonies were, after all, still part of the British Empire. It would be nearly a century before the American Revolution and the beginnings of the United States of America. The Members of Parliament in London could see no reason why those British colonists across the Atlantic should be competing unfairly against shippers who sailed from London. There ought to be a law against it, they decided. So they passed a number of laws.

In essence the Acts of Trade and Navigation required the shippers of the North American colonies to trade only with England and the other English colonies. Some of the laws, in fact, had been passed as early as 1660, when William Kidd was a young man. The only way a New York merchant could purchase something from the French or Dutch islands of the West Indies was by way of London. In short, the West Indies trading business was to be kept in the family. And the head of the family was in London.

In New York the merchants and the skippers reacted with anger and rebellion. They could not afford to send their little trading sloops across the Atlantic instead of down to the islands. They could not afford the higher prices they would have to pay in England for goods which they had been buying more cheaply at the source, in the islands. So the New Yorkers and the other colonists broke London's law. They protested against the Acts of Trade and Navigation. But in the meantime, knowing their protests would get them nowhere, they simply ignored the Acts. They did it by smuggling.

Trading sloops sailed silently out at night, slipping past the British coastal patrols and setting the familiar course for the West Indies. Back they came with their cargoes, ghosting into harbor at night. His Majesty's customs officials were bribed to look the other way when the goods were stored in warehouses and sold on the markets, just as they had been sold before the Acts were passed.

And once the New Yorkers discovered that they could get away with breaking one law, they were tempted to break another. If you can be a successful smuggler, why not be an even more successful pirate? So it was that more and more American ships simply sailed out to capture merchant vessels, take their cargo, and bring it into New York—past the same patrols and bribing the same customs officers.

New York became even more prosperous, and even more of an outlaw city. And because of a money shortage in the colonies, the pirates, with their silver and specie, could not only bribe the lower officials in the customs, but also make life comfortable and luxurious for the highest officers of the city. Benjamin Fletcher, the governor of New York, was soon suspected of dealing with the pirates. So were the governors of the other port towns of the colonies.

Governor Fletcher all but admitted that he had a secret agreement with the pirates. He made friends with them, entertained them at dinner, and drove them around in his carriage. Some New Yorkers claimed that the governor had a flat fee for landing permits: £100 per pirate. And there were rumors that he had a financial interest in several pirate ventures. Certainly the governor lived well on what was supposed to be a modest salary from London. He even bragged about his wife's madras silks which, he said, once belonged to a princess in India. How had they got to New York? The governor declined to say.

Captain Kidd could not have continued to trade among the islands without some smuggling. But he was not a pirate. In fact, he had been commissioned by the colonial authorities to chase pirates off the New England coast. Moreover, down in the West Indies, he had had an encounter that had embittered him against pirates for some years to come.

He had gone ashore on the island of St. Martin for

the night and waked in the morning to find that his ship had been taken from him. The crew had mutinied in his absence and had sailed the ship away. The leader of the mutiny had been a rebellious crew member named Robert Culliford, who had talked the rest of the crew into turning the vessel into a pirate ship. Kidd would cross paths with Robert Culliford again.

Pirates were not the only thing troubling England and the English colonies. Throughout the last part of the seventeenth century England and France were fighting and squabbling with each other. This on-off war would last for over a century. During one of his voyages to the West Indies Captain Kidd had helped a British force drive away a group of six French naval vessels that were besieging a British island. Because of this, when the governor of the Leeward Islands heard that Captain Kidd had lost his ship, he presented Kidd with a new brigantine. In gratitude Captain Kidd named her *Antigua,* after the major island of the group. Then he sailed her back to New York.

And there he made a big mistake.

The rumors and suspicions about New York's Governor Fletcher had begun to worry the authorities in London. Besides, there had been some elections in New York, and London had received complaints that the elections had been managed badly, if not dishonestly, by the governor. As one of the most respectable merchants of the city, Captain Kidd was asked if he would come to London to testify in an inquest into the election. Partly because he enjoyed sailing his new brigantine *Antigua,* Captain Kidd agreed to go. That was the mistake.

In London that summer was another prominent New Yorker. Colonel Robert Livingston was the sort of person who openly admitted, "I would rather be called Knave Livingston than a poor man." His business dealings in New York had never been proved outrageously dishonest. But he was not the type anyone wanted to trust too far.

Colonel Livingston did have a pleasant personality, and he knew how to use it. He was in London partly because he had heard a rumor that New York's Governor Fletcher might be recalled. When he reached London, he found that he had heard aright. A new governor had been appointed. He was one of the most influential men in King William's government. His name was Richard Coote, but he was generally known by his title: the Earl of Bellomont.

Colonel Livingston wasted no time in arranging to meet and ingratiate himself with the new governor. For his part, Lord Bellomont was pleased by the flattering attention of his visitor from New York. And it happened that before he left to take up his new position, Lord Bellomont had a piece of business to transact. Colonel Livingston could help him. Did the Colonel know of a reliable New York captain who might be entrusted with a delicate mission? Were there any honest skippers left in New York? If so, how could one be located?

Colonel Livingston replied immediately that he not only knew of one but counted him as a friend. And by a surprising coincidence the man was in London at the moment. Livingston would bring him to meet his lordship. The man's name was William Kidd.

The Mysterious Syndicate

Captain Kidd was surrounded by strangers. He had not been to London for years. So he was pleased to see a familiar face from New York. When Colonel Livingston invited him to meet the new governor of New York, Kidd was happy to go along. Taking a carriage to Lord Bellomont's town house in Dover Street, they announced themselves to the butler and were shown into the paneled library.

Lord Bellomont was pompous and portly but businesslike. He wasted little time in small talk and quickly got to the matter at hand. He and some friends were planning to mount a pirate-chasing expedition, and his lordship would be pleased if Captain Kidd would take the command.

There was, of course, a lot more to it than that. And as Lord Bellomont talked on about the project, Captain Kidd began to realize how ambitious it was.

Pirates in the New World were indeed a problem for the British government. But many of these pirates were rapidly becoming an even greater problem in another part of the world. Halfway around the globe from New York they were causing London a lot more trouble. In fact, they were endangering the richest new source of trade that Britain had ever had.

Out to the east, beyond Europe and Africa and the Persian Gulf, British traders had discovered a vast source of wealth. The huge subcontinent of India had become a central market for all the treasures of the Orient—diamonds, rubies, and "Arab gold," madras, muslins, and silks. All these riches came to India, ready to be bought by visiting traders and shipped to the West to be resold at enormous profit. So great were the prospects of this trade that a big shipping combine, the East India Company, had been formed just to take advantage of it. The East India Company had already begun to pay off handsomely. But now it was in deep trouble. And all because of the pirates.

Like birds of prey the pirates of the New World had

followed the traders down around the Cape of Good Hope at the bottom of Africa, and up into the Indian Ocean, where the merchant fleets came out of the rich ports of India. And the pirates had attacked not only the traders from Europe but the Indian vessels as well. Finally one of them had, in one attack, threatened all of England's trade in the Orient.

India was ruled at the time by an absolute monarch, the Great Mogul. Any trade with India depended on his pleasure. For a while the East India Company's dealings with India were profitable enough for the Great Mogul so that business was brisk. But soon the pirates began to make the traders' life difficult. And then one pirate nearly brought all trade to a stop.

His name was Henry Every. He had had a successful career of piracy in the Atlantic but, as richer possibilities beckoned, Every followed the other pirates down around the tip of Africa and up into the Indian Ocean.

Henry Every had a reputation as a lucky pirate. But he had rarely had such good luck as on this occasion. In the Indian Ocean he came upon a ship which turned out to be no ordinary merchantman. She was one of the Great Mogul's own ships, *Gunsway*. She carried members of his family, plus an entire cargo of jewels and coin. *Gunsway* was poorly defended. After an uneven two-hour battle, her captain surrendered.

Henry Every captured all the jewels, 100,000 pieces of eight, and one of the Mogul's women relatives, and sailed off to the island of Madagascar.

When the news reached the Great Mogul, he announced that unless the British caught Henry Every and brought him to justice, every British trading post in India would be closed down and the British traders sent home. In short, the great East India Company would be put out of business, and England's richest source of trade would be no more.

That is why, in August 1695, Captain William Kidd found himself in the library of Lord Bellomont.

Lord Bellomont explained to Captain Kidd and Colonel Livingston that the pirates must be driven out of the Indian Ocean. His lordship and some friends were accordingly mounting this expedition to chase them down. Captain Kidd, Bellomont thought, seemed the perfect man to command such an expedition.

After recovering from the surprise, Captain Kidd replied as courteously as he could. He agreed that it was a worthy venture. Someone certainly should go after Every and the other pirates. But he pointed out that there were many captains who could head such an expedition. New York was full of experienced skippers, many of whom would leap at the chance of

an adventure like this. He was flattered at the suggestion that he could be the choice of Lord Bellomont. But he was sure that his lordship, when he went to New York, would find candidates better suited to the task.

Years later Captain Kidd still recalled his surprise at Lord Bellomont's reply. In a polite but firm tone, his lordship made himself clear: Captain Kidd did not appear to understand. He was not being *asked* if he would like to command the expedition; he was being *requested* to do it. Lord Bellomont was the new governor. He could select whom he wanted. Captain Kidd was the man he had chosen. And if Captain Kidd doubted the power of the new governor, he would shortly find out he was wrong.

There was, for one thing, Captain Kidd's favorite ship, *Antigua*, anchored in the stream below London. If the captain wished to keep *Antigua*, he would do as he was told. If he refused, he must realize that he was defying the newly appointed authority of New York and New England. Did the captain really believe that he could say "no" to the governor and then return to New York as if nothing had happened? Did he think that he could ever send another ship out of New York? Didn't he understand all the problems he would face if he defied the representative of the King?

Wasn't Captain Kidd ready to reconsider?

Captain Kidd admitted that perhaps he was.

Officially it looked like a normal arrangement. Captain William Kidd was duly commissioned by His Majesty William III to search for and capture any "pirates, freebooters and sea rovers…which you shall meet with." He was to bring the pirates, along with their captured ships, into New York or any other American or British port.

There was a second commission. This one authorized and directed him to seize all "ships, vessels and goods belonging to the French King and his subjects." Not only was it a pirate-chasing expedition; it was a privateering venture as well.

England was still at war with France. In such wars at that time the governments used an ingenious method of increasing their forces by employing private vessels to help fight the war. Besides the regular naval forces, they issued "licenses" to merchant captains to become private warriors. With a privateer's commission any captain and crew were entitled to chase and capture any vessel belonging to the enemy. Though the names sounded alike, there was a big difference between a pirate and a privateer. The privateer carried a commission which legally entitled him to capture certain ships. The pirate carried no commission and captured any ship he could. Often the pirate tried to pretend he was a privateer. But if he carried no commission, or if he attacked a non-enemy ship, he was a pirate. In short, the privateer was legal—the pirate was an outlaw.

So Captain Kidd was a licensed pirate-chaser and a licensed enemy-chaser. But beneath the official commissions was an unofficial conspiracy.

Few ships' captains could afford to outfit privateering expeditions by themselves. What they did was either band together or sell shares to a number of wealthy investors. The money was used to build or purchase the privateering vessel, arm it, and buy the provisions for an extended voyage. Then the investors waited for results. When the privateer captured an enemy vessel, the vessel and its goods were sold at auction and the proceeds were divided. An investor who had contributed a large amount received a larger share. The captain received a small share if he had invested no money himself, a larger share if he had. And a portion was set aside for the crew. So if the privateer was successful, the investors, the captain, and the crew were paid handsomely. If the privateer was unsuccessful, they got little or nothing. The phrase at the time was: "No prey, no pay."

This was the arrangement presented to Captain Kidd. A group of Englishmen had agreed to invest in this pirate-chasing and privateering expedition. But in this case there was an important difference. Lord Bellomont told Captain Kidd and Colonel Livingston that his lordship and some other Englishmen were backing the project. But Bellomont was carefully silent about who the other Englishmen were. The reason was that these other investors were members of the British government.

There was no law against members of the government investing in a privateering voyage. But this was more than just a privateering voyage. And these men were not behaving entirely honorably when they invested in it. They were the King's ministers and they were using their influence and inside information to get in on a profitable deal. The pirate-chasing part of the expedition was a new venture. Britain wanted to rid the Indian Ocean of pirates. In the process, a few British ministers proposed to make some money out of it.

In fact, not only had King William III been persuaded to lend his Great Seal to a money-making venture—he had been included in the deal. The King was to get ten percent of the profits.

Lord Bellomont knew enough about British politics in those days to realize what a howl would go up if it were known that the King and his ministers were using the privilege of the Crown to make money for themselves. So he organized this syndicate secretly and kept the members' names to himself. The members included the Chancellor of the Exchequer, the Secretary of State, and one of the chief admirals of the Royal Navy. But this was not revealed until later.

So far as Captain Kidd knew, he was dealing with Lord Bellomont and a group of "silent partners." They drove a hard bargain. The syndicate was to receive sixty percent of the proceeds from the voyage. Captain Kidd and Colonel Livingston were to receive fifteen percent between them. The remaining twenty-five percent was to be divided among the crew. This was far less than most privateering crews received, but Bellomont refused to cut back his percentage. At one point he even asked Kidd to see if he could persuade his crew to take less than twenty-five percent.

For his small share of the profits Captain Kidd was expected to put up a part of the investment. How? Why, there was his brigantine *Antigua*. He wouldn't be needing her, Bellomont explained, because the syndicate was providing a larger ship for the expedition. His lordship made it sound as if they were doing Kidd a favor.

Captain Kidd knew he had no choice. He could only accept his two commissions, take command of the new ship, and do his best to accomplish the mission.

Then he could return to New York and retire, perhaps with a fair amount of money if his voyage were successful.

But he did insist on one concession. He decided to take his new pirate-chasing ship to New York for a last reunion with Sarah and Elizabeth, whether the syndicate liked it or not, before he set out on his long and perilous voyage.

The new vessel's name was to be *Adventure Galley*. She was still on the stocks, unfinished, in Castle's Yard at Deptford, near Greenwich, a few miles down the Thames from London. Kidd went down to look her over. She was a big ship, nearly three hundred tons. And her sides were pierced for thirty guns. She could capture nearly all the Indian Ocean pirates if she sailed as well as she looked.

But before she was launched, Captain Kidd had begun to learn the ways of shipbuilders—and provisioners and recruiters—in London in 1695. Green wood was being used in *Adventure Galley*'s construction. Kidd knew it was not seasoned enough. It would swell and buckle once the ship was launched. She would leak—not just for the first few days when any new ship could be expected to leak—possibly all the way across the Atlantic, with the men working the pumps day and night.

Captain Kidd complained to the shipbuilder. The shipbuilder paid no attention. When Kidd carried his complaint further, he found that nothing could be done. The shipbuilder had bribed the inspector to approve the wood, and the inspector had no intention of reversing his approval and making an enemy of the shipbuilder. There would be other ships, and other bribes, and other approvals. It had gone on like this for years, and it would go on like this for years to come.

Captain Kidd inspected the food as it was delivered. It was already rotten. The other supplies were fewer than had been paid for. But he quickly found that the suppliers had also bribed the right people—to look the other way, to miscount, to stow everything below without checking too carefully. This "understanding" had gone on too long for a mere captain to upset it now. So Captain Kidd found that he had little to say about how well his ship was built or how she was provisioned.

But he did have some help in finding men for his crew. The East India Company was most concerned over the pirate attacks in the Indian Ocean, and most interested in *Adventure Galley*'s success. And the East India Company was one of the most powerful organizations in England. A director of the company offered to assist Kidd with the recruiting. With his help the men who formed *Adventure Galley*'s crew turned out to be a lot better than the ship they would man. Edmund Harrison, the director, had his own peculiar reasons for making some of the selections he did. He ruled out anyone from the colonies, explaining that they might turn pirate. Only true-blue Englishmen were permitted to sign aboard.

The might of the East India Company was such that men for *Adventure Galley* appeared from everywhere. Captain Kidd had learned enough of the ways of London by now so he did not inquire too closely into where the men had been found, or what might have been done to them to persuade them to sign aboard. He simply followed the "suggestions" of Mr. Harrison and was thankful for every man he got.

So finally *Adventure Galley* was launched and her men piped aboard. She leaked as Kidd had expected. But as her seams swelled in the water, the leaks became trickles. And it was too soon for the men to start complaining about the food. *Adventure Galley*'s lines were cast off and the sails were hoisted to fill with the wind. In late February 1696 the ship moved downriver, heading for the open sea.

Out at the Nore, where the river reached the ocean, lying across her course as if waiting for her, was a British man-of-war.

4

ADVENTURE GALLEY SETS SAIL

She was H.M.S. *Duchess* under Captain Stuart, and she signaled *Adventure Galley* to heave to. Captain Kidd would have preferred to slip around the warship. But he realized that he could not get away. He had no idea how fast *Adventure Galley* was. He had a new and untried crew who had had no time to train together. Besides, he should have no reason to fear any British man-of-war. He carried two royal commissions, embossed with the Great Seal of the King. So he hove to and awaited the boarding party from *Duchess*.

Duchess' jolly boat came across the narrow distance between the two ships. While the oarsmen waited below, the young officer from *Duchess* climbed aboard, presented his compliments to Captain Kidd—and asked for half of his crew.

This was how the Royal Navy found crewmen for its ships in the seventeenth century. The navy was famous for poor pay, disgusting food, and the lash for anyone who complained. Nobody but a fool would volunteer for the navy. Sailors were found by raiding the public houses of London, Liverpool, and other port cities. And by "the Press."

Nothing was more feared by the young men of Britain and the colonies than the Press. Gangs of navy bullyboys grabbed any young man they could lay hands on, whisked him aboard a boat and out to a navy ship. If he resisted, he woke up aboard ship next morning with a clotted wound where the press gang had clubbed him. Often a young wife would wait all night for her husband to come home from an errand. When he did not return she would begin to fear that he had been grabbed by the Press. Sure enough, months later she would receive a letter from him in far-off Zanzibar, telling her that he was now a seaman in His Majesty's navy. And only the good Lord knew when she and the children would see him again.

The Press worked at sea as well as on land. Captain Kidd, like any other captain who sailed the seas in the seventeenth century, had seen the Press in action before.

And here, at the beginning of his voyage, he was confronted with it again.

But this time he had assumed that his own men would be safe. After all, he was in command of an expedition sponsored by the powerful Lord Bellomont. He carried two royal commissions. The Royal Navy never "pressed" men from one naval vessel to another. Surely they could not take any of his crew from *Adventure Galley*.

So he was shocked and outraged when the young naval officer paid no attention to his arguments or to his royal commissions, but simply cut out the best men from *Adventure Galley*'s crew and had them rowed across to the man-of-war.

Captain Kidd sent an angry complaint to Lord Bellomont and the syndicate. Within a few days he had the satisfaction of seeing some of his men returned to him. *Duchess* had been on her way home for refit, and orders went from the syndicate to Captain Stuart to return the men he had taken from *Adventure Galley*. Counting the men who were returned to him, Captain Kidd saw that he did not get all of them back, nor did he get the best of them. But at least he had enough crew to set sail again. He could recruit more men in New York, where he knew the city better than he did London. So, reluctantly, he put out again.

Out on the Atlantic he sighted his first prize. At first she appeared to be an ordinary fishing schooner rolling along in the mid-ocean swells. But then Kidd noticed that she flew the French flag. Evidently she was not a pirate. But one of Kidd's commissions directed him to capture any vessel belonging to France, as long as France and England were at war.

It was a quick and simple matter to swoop down on the little schooner and capture her. She carried salt and fishing tackle, and she was bound for Newfoundland. Captain Kidd sent a prize crew aboard her, and the schooner followed *Adventure Galley* into New York harbor.

In proper order, as specified in his commission, Captain Kidd handed the schooner over to the Vice Admiralty Court in New York, and the vessel and her contents were sold at auction. The sale brought £350. The syndicate's percentage was forwarded to London, and Kidd set aside the remainder to pay for provisions for the voyage that *Adventure Galley* was about to undertake. It was a good omen. *Adventure Galley* had made her first kill.

Sarah Kidd could not be expected to approve of her husband's new venture. But wives in those days, especially captains' wives, obeyed their husbands and abided by their decisions. Sarah Kidd realized that her husband had no choice either, in this case. So she did what she could to help him enjoy the few weeks he would have at home before undertaking his long voyage.

There was also a lot of work to be done. The seventy men Kidd had brought from England could handle *Adventure Galley*'s miles of rigging. But many more would be needed to sail her and work her guns at the same time. So Captain Kidd's first order of business was to recruit more men.

He sent his recruiters out among the wharves, saloons, and boarding houses along the waterfront. They returned with bad news. The Press had been at work in New York too, and few good sailors had escaped the navy's dragnet. The men whom the recruiters found were not interested in serving aboard *Adventure Galley*.

One good reason was the twenty-five percent share which the agreement with the syndicate provided for the crew. The seamen along the New York docks turned away from Kidd's recruiters when they heard about it. Few of them said so, but everyone knew that on any of the pirate ships they could get more than fifty percent. Some pirate captains offered as much as seventy-five percent.

Piracy was illegal, and *Adventure Galley*'s pirate-chasing expedition was legal. But pirates had been escaping punishment in New York for years, thanks to Governor Fletcher. *Adventure Galley*'s voyage seemed as risky as any pirate voyage. A sailor could get killed as quickly in a battle with pirates as on a pirate ship itself. Why risk your life for twenty-five percent when you could make more as a pirate?

After days of unsuccessful recruiting, Captain Kidd decided that he had to raise the crew's share. He told his recruiters to offer as much as sixty percent. He could explain it to Lord Bellomont later. If he stuck by the twenty-five percent share, there wouldn't be any expedition. Better a smaller share for himself and the syndicate than nothing at all.

When he offered the new share, some recruits began to come forward. Watching them sign the papers—many of them with an "X" because they could not write their names—Captain Kidd was far from relieved. They were a lot worse than the men he had signed on in England. Many of them looked more like pirates than pirate-chasers. He wondered if he could keep them under control, or if he might lose *Adventure Galley* the way he had lost his ship in the West Indies. But these men were the best he could get. They would have to do.

There was much more work before *Adventure Galley* could be ready. More provisions had to be purchased

to replace some of the rotten stuff provided in London. Salt beef, casks of water, and barrels of rum were trundled down the wharf, hoisted aboard, and stowed in the hold. Cannonballs, powder, and flints were loaded, to be ready for the battles to come. Slowly *Adventure Galley* was outfitted for her voyage.

And finally Captain Kidd could enjoy a last few days with his family. With Sarah and their two-year-old daughter Elizabeth he rode up to their vacation house, in what was then open country and is now 74th Street. And when they returned to the big brick town house, he walked down to the Customs House and the busy piers to see how *Adventure Galley*'s outfitting had gone.

Her crew now numbered 150. Nearly all her gear was in place, and the provisions were stowed. It was time to go.

On September 6, 1696, Sarah and Elizabeth came with him to the wharf on the East River, at the foot of Wall Street, for the last time. A brief good-by kiss to both of them, and Captain Kidd stepped aboard *Adventure Galley* and walked aft to the quarterdeck.

His first mate waited for orders. Looking out across the river and aloft at *Adventure Galley*'s yardarms swarming with men, Captain Kidd gave the command to set sails. In a rush the sails spread to the breeze. Captain Kidd gave the next order, and the lines were cast off from the wharf. With a last wave to the little crowd on the shore, Captain Kidd gave his directions to the helmsman.

Adventure Galley moved slowly out into the stream and gathered speed as the wind and current eased her downriver. The wharf receded and the people became specks. He could no longer make out Sarah and Elizabeth. *Adventure Galley* sailed down the harbor and out past the Narrows. Then the sea began to take hold of the ship—lifting her and rolling her as her bow pointed eastward, toward the coast of Africa, the Cape of Good Hope, Madagascar, and pirate country.

East to Madagascar

As soon as land disappeared astern, it was time to make things shipshape. Sailors were divided into watches to man the ship twenty-four hours a day. The guns were run out and gunners were trained until they could load, fire, clean, and reload without pause. *Adventure Galley*'s life—and the lives of her men—would depend upon how fast they could work her guns. Driven before the prevailing winds and helped along by the Atlantic currents, *Adventure Galley* was running eastward toward Africa when the lookout sighted a sail.

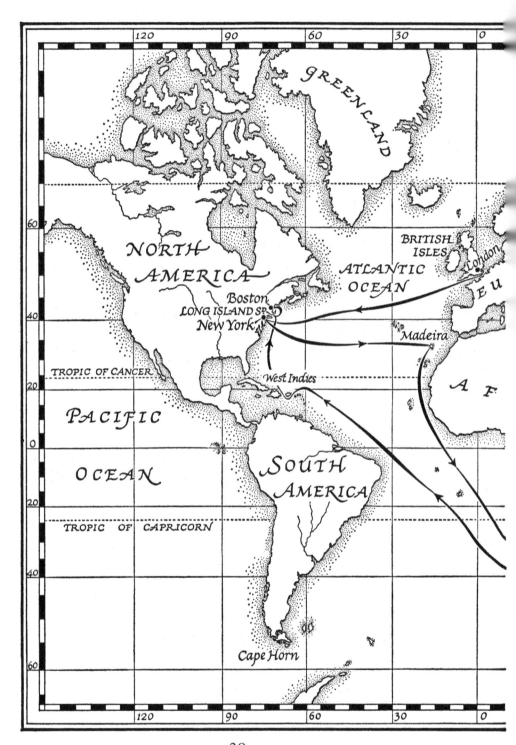

5

East to Madagascar

As soon as land disappeared astern, it was time to make things shipshape. Sailors were divided into watches to man the ship twenty-four hours a day. The guns were run out and gunners were trained until they could load, fire, clean, and reload without pause. *Adventure Galley*'s life—and the lives of her men—would depend upon how fast they could work her guns. Driven before the prevailing winds and helped along by the Atlantic currents, *Adventure Galley* was running eastward toward Africa when the lookout sighted a sail.

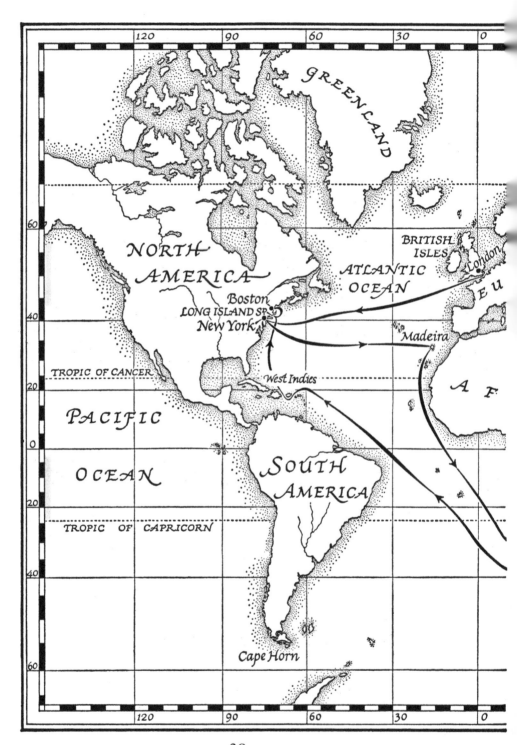

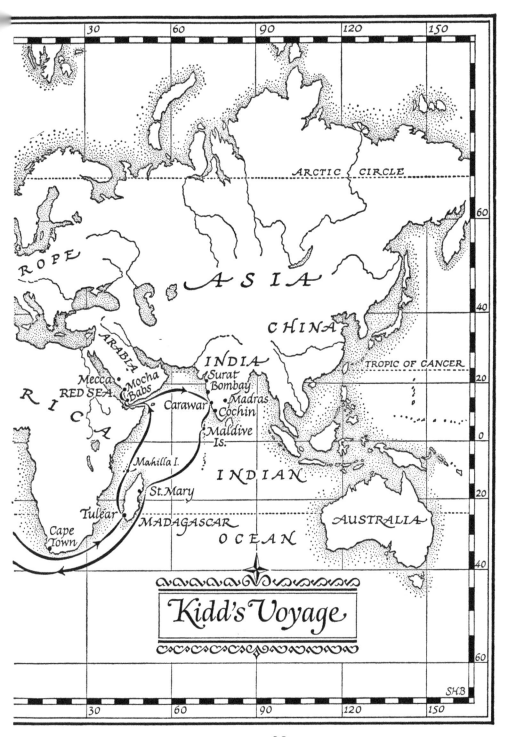

Captain Kidd sent *Adventure Galley* after her. The gunners moved to their stations. Slowly they overtook their prize. As they came closer they could make her out better. She was a brigantine and no match for *Adventure Galley*. But when they finally came within hailing distance, she identified herself. She was from Bermuda, a British colony.

Since she was neither a pirate nor a Frenchman, they could not seize her. Instead the two vessels sailed in company until they reached the island of Madeira. Putting into Madeira's calm harbor and dropping anchor, Captain Kidd sent a boat ashore for fresh water, green vegetables, and other provisions. Madeira was a pleasant port, with friendly people, flower-covered hillsides, and fine wines that would later become famous all over the world. But *Adventure Galley*'s business lay farther eastward. So Captain Kidd took her back onto the Atlantic and on toward the Cape of Good Hope.

They were within six hundred miles of the Cape when the lookout called down again. This time he had sighted not one but four ships. Captain Kidd approached them with more caution than he had used in chasing down the single brigantine.

Again the ships were neither pirate nor French. In fact, they were British men-of-war.

Captain Kidd remembered H.M.S. *Duchess* and the

Press. But again he was not sure he could escape. If he tried to run for it, he might find himself in greater trouble than if he faced up to the British commander. So he sailed up to join the men-of-war. They hove to and waited for him.

One of the warships signaled an invitation, and Kidd had himself rowed across to her. On board he was greeted by Captain Thomas Warren of His Majesty's Navy. Kidd introduced himself, explained his mission, and showed Captain Warren his commissions. To his relief Captain Warren welcomed him and invited him to sail in company with the men-of-war.

For a week *Adventure Galley* and the four British ships ran down along the coast toward the Cape and the bottom of the African continent. The two largest ships were H.M.S. *Tiger* and *Advice;* the smaller two were escorts. In the custom of His Majesty's Navy, formal dinner was served aboard *Tiger* and *Advice* every evening, and Captain Kidd enjoyed the luxury of leisurely evenings in the wardroom being waited on by orderlies. Then one evening, over the brandy and cigars, Captain Warren mentioned that he might need a few more crewmen.

Captain Kidd was ready for him. He replied that he thought he could spare some men, and proposed that he send them over the next day. Then he returned to *Adventure Galley* for the night.

Instead of retiring, he waited until a few hours before dawn. The wind had died and the five ships were barely moving. Quietly Kidd ordered his men into the boats. Softly they set to towing *Adventure Galley* away from the other ships. By dawn, in a flat calm, it was too late for the British warships to chase him. *Adventure Galley* was nearly over the horizon and too far away to be caught.

Captain Kidd had planned to put into Cape Town, Africa's most southern port, for more fresh water and provisions. But now he decided against it. The British warships would certainly come in there looking for him, and there would be no escape then. So *Adventure Galley* sailed on around the Cape of Good Hope, and set her course north and east—for Madagascar.

The island lay like an enormous whale in the Indian Ocean, more than two hundred miles off the coast of East Africa. It was late January of 1697 before *Adventure Galley*'s men sighted her long, low coastline. Running before the steady southeast trade wind, *Adventure Galley* moved slowly along the coast. Palm trees, pines, and strange tall tree trunks with bushy tops grew along the shores. Far in the background the plains rose in tiers to a plateau broken by mountains. Down from the plateau, through deep green valleys, rivers ran toward the sea. But always they emptied into lagoons or deltas, instead of a harbor or a bay that could provide shelter for a ship.

It was the rainy season, and *Adventure Galley* was periodically drenched by sudden, howling squalls, which were quickly followed by the hot tropical sun. Occasionally a brilliant butterfly would flutter onto a yardarm or the ship's rail, its wings pulsating as if exhausted by the long flight. The musky smell of land was enticing, after so many months at sea. But not until they had sailed almost five hundred miles along the coast did a harbor finally come into sight.

On the charts the place was called Telere (Toliara today). In the same harbor was another settlement named St. Augustine. Here, Captain Kidd had been told, bands of pirates had established their Indian Ocean bases. Madagascar was the perfect pirate outpost, a few days' sail from the rich Malabar Coast and athwart the sea lanes which the East India Company had to follow from India to England. Yet Madagascar, one thousand miles long, was too big for the Royal Navy to occupy or police. So the pirates had taken over most of Madagascar's few harbors, driving the natives inland and fortifying their own settlements. Madagascar was pirate country. Captain Kidd expected at last to find his prey here.

But he found no pirates at all. In the harbor was a brigantine from Barbados. There was also a wrecked French ship, evidently driven aground by one of the squalls. But there were no pirate ships.

Most of the pirates, apparently, either were off prowling for merchantmen or had moved their activities to harbors along the east coast, on the other side of the island. If Henry Every had come in here at all, he had long since moved on.

Kidd decided to set out looking for pirates on the open sea. First he sent a boat over to the French wreck. The men returned with a surprise—a small cache of gold. Under the regulations of his privateer's commission, Kidd appropriated the gold. According to their articles, sixty percent would be shared between the crew, so this was a small boost for their morale. It wasn't much, but it was the first valuable find in half a year.

Then—sails set again—*Adventure Galley* moved out of the harbor. The palm-hut village disappeared behind the headland, and she headed north again, looking for pirates. Running before the trade winds, occasionally battered by squalls, *Adventure Galley* sailed north to Johanna Island, where Captain Kidd looked for any hiding pirates. There were none. Off west they sailed to Mahilla Island. No pirates.

And now *Adventure Galley*'s men were suffering from more than low spirits. Many of the men were physically ill as well. Despite the stops at Madeira and at these Indian Ocean islands, the crew was succumbing to that scourge of the seventeenth century sailing ship—scurvy. The disease was caused by a diet of too much salt meat with too few green vegetables or fruit. Apparently the crew had not eaten enough at the islands to make up for the vitamin deficiency in their diet.

One by one they complained of bleeding gums, then weakness. Then they began to faint. Some were unable to get out of their hammocks when it was time to go on watch. Others dropped on deck. Some were able to climb the rigging, only to lose hold and come thumping down to a bloody death on deck. Day after day there were burials at sea. *Adventure Galley*'s sailmaker sewed the body into a tarpaulin. Lead shot from the ship's guns was poured into the feet of the tarpaulin to weigh it down. A brief service was held at the ship's rail, and the heavy bundle was hoisted over the side. As the men looked back, nothing but a row of bubbles showed where their shipmate was sinking to the bottom of the sea, to become food for sharks.

Watching these burials, and checking *Adventure Galley*'s slowing progress day by day, Captain Kidd decided to go ashore at Mahilla Island and careen the ship.

Adventure Galley was in worse shape than most of her crew. After months in tropical waters her bottom was fouled and dragging her down. Teredo worms had riddled her planks with holes. Barnacles clung in thick patches, coated by green slime. Long trails of weed streamed astern. Captain Kidd estimated that, except in a blow, *Adventure Galley* could make only half her normal speed. She would be no match for a fleeing pirate. It was time for cleaning her hull.

He searched out a shelving shore on the island and sailed up to the beach until the ship crunched onto the bottom. Then the heavy work of careening began. Everything that could not be secured aboard had to go ashore. The cannon were dismantled from the deck and swung by block and tackle into the boats, then manhandled onto the beach. Spars were sent down and stacked ashore. Ship's stores and ammunition were laboriously ferried to the beach. Even the hammocks were unloaded, to be slung between trees on shore, where the crew would live while the careening went on.

Now the heavy lines were run from *Adventure Galley*'s mast top to windlasses on the shore, and the men strained to haul in the lines. Leaning into the spokes of the windlasses, they sweated in the ninety-degree heat and the melting humidity. Gradually the big ship creaked over onto her side. Other crewmen shoved massive wedges under her keel to hold her in place. Then they went to work scraping off the growth and weed, cleaning and plugging the thousands of teredo holes, and covering *Adventure Galley*'s hull with a new coat of tar. The careening took weeks, and all through that time the men worked amidst swarms of mosquitoes.

Soon the effect of the mosquito bites was felt. Malaria, the disease of the tropics, infected one man after another. First came fever, then chills, until each victim was reduced to chattering delirium. Beyond the beach a new graveyard began to fill. By the time *Adventure Galley* was finally ready to sail again, her original crew of 150 had been reduced to 100.

Those who survived were desperate men. They had watched their shipmates die of scurvy and malaria. They had been away from home for eight months. In all that time they had not seen, much less captured, a pirate ship. They had only the small cache of gold from the French wreck. Under the articles they had signed, they had almost nothing to show for more than half a year of miserable existence, hard labor, and the perils of disease.

So as *Adventure Galley,* cleaned and refitted, sailed from Mahilla Island and set her new course, many of decided to go ashore at Mahilla Island and careen the ship.

Adventure Galley was in worse shape than most of her crew. After months in tropical waters her bottom was fouled and dragging her down. Teredo worms had riddled her planks with holes. Barnacles clung in thick patches, coated by green slime. Long trails of weed streamed astern. Captain Kidd estimated that, except in a blow, *Adventure Galley* could make only half her normal speed. She would be no match for a fleeing pirate. It was time for cleaning her hull.

He searched out a shelving shore on the island and sailed up to the beach until the ship crunched onto the bottom. Then the heavy work of careening began. Everything that could not be secured aboard had to go ashore. The cannon were dismantled from the deck and swung by block and tackle into the boats, then manhandled onto the beach. Spars were sent down and stacked ashore. Ship's stores and ammunition were laboriously ferried to the beach. Even the hammocks were unloaded, to be slung between trees on shore, where the crew would live while the careening went on.

Now the heavy lines were run from *Adventure Galley*'s mast top to windlasses on the shore, and the men strained to haul in the lines. Leaning into the spokes of the windlasses, they sweated in the ninety-degree heat and the melting humidity. Gradually the big ship creaked over onto her side. Other crewmen shoved massive wedges under her keel to hold her in place. Then they went to work scraping off the growth and weed, cleaning and plugging the thousands of teredo holes, and covering *Adventure Galley*'s hull with a new coat of tar. The careening took weeks, and all through that time the men worked amidst swarms of mosquitoes.

Soon the effect of the mosquito bites was felt. Malaria, the disease of the tropics, infected one man after another. First came fever, then chills, until each victim was reduced to chattering delirium. Beyond the beach a new graveyard began to fill. By the time *Adventure Galley* was finally ready to sail again, her original crew of 150 had been reduced to 100.

Those who survived were desperate men. They had watched their shipmates die of scurvy and malaria. They had been away from home for eight months. In all that time they had not seen, much less captured, a pirate ship. They had only the small cache of gold from the French wreck. Under the articles they had signed, they had almost nothing to show for more than half a year of miserable existence, hard labor, and the perils of disease.

So as *Adventure Galley*, cleaned and refitted, sailed from Mahilla Island and set her new course, many of her crewmen were muttering to each other that they had had enough of pirate-chasing. They should capture the next ship they sighted, whether she was a pirate, or a Frenchman, or an innocent victim.

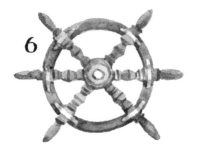

Action at Sea

Adventure Galley's course lay northeast, along Africa's coast. Rounding Cape Guardafui, Captain Kidd took the ship into the Gulf of Aden and west to the islands known as the Babs.

The Babs nestled in the narrow entrance where the Gulf of Aden turned into the Red Sea. Here was the bottleneck through which the richest fleets had to pass. They were called the Mocha fleets because the port city of Mocha was the last stop in the Red Sea before setting out across the Arabian Sea and Indian Ocean to India. On the Red Sea was Mecca, the holy center for all Muslims. To Mecca went vast treasures of jewels and gold from the devout Muslim potentates of India and other Asian kingdoms. So the Babs presented a favorite hiding place for pirates.

But this time there were no pirates in the Babs. For three weeks *Adventure Galley* poked into every cove and harbor looking for them, with no success. Then, just as Captain Kidd prepared to move on, his luck suddenly turned.

Out from the Red Sea and through the narrow passageway past the Babs came the grandest flotilla *Adventure Galley*'s men had ever seen. As far as the eye could make out, off over the horizon, the line of ships spread before them. It was like a sea of white canvas as the big ships moved slowly toward the islands—right across the path of *Adventure Galley* and her hungry men.

Captain Kidd knew that these Mocha fleets often carried French cargoes. They would not be flying the French flag. More likely some of the Moorish vessels would be carrying French passes, commissioning them to transport goods for France. If he could not find any pirates, he could at least capture one of these ships, under the provisions of his privateering commission. He could pick out a likely victim, capture her, and inspect her papers. If they included a French pass, he had a legitimate prize. If there were no French pass, he could let her go, and pick out another ship from this huge fleet.

The weather conditions were just right. There was a light breeze, and *Adventure Galley*, with her newly cleaned bottom, could run down her victims at will. Studying the stately oncoming armada, Captain Kidd selected a Moorish vessel near *Adventure Galley*. To his eager crew, watching impatiently from the deck, he gave the order to attack.

Flying no colors, only a broad pennant which fluttered weakly in the light breeze, *Adventure Galley* slipped out of her hiding place and moved alongside the convoy. Perhaps the other captains would mistake her for one of the ships in the fleet, until she came close enough and it was too late. While *Adventure Galley* moved slowly toward the Moorish ship, Captain Kidd kept an eye on the rest of the convoy. Were any of the captains becoming suspicious? This was the notorious pirate ambush, the gauntlet every fleet had to run before reaching the open waters of the Gulf of Aden and the Arabian Sea. So every skipper would be on the lookout. And, most important, where were the warships protecting the convoy?

As he watched, *Adventure Galley* approached her quarry. Now the wind weakened even more and all but died. Across the water there appeared to be no waves or ruffles to indicate more wind. *Adventure Galley*'s pennant hung limply from the masthead. Everything —*Adventure Galley*, the Moorish vessel, and all the other ships—slowed, halted, and seemed suspended on the ocean, their yards swinging and their sails slatting as the waveless swells rocked them back and forth.

Captain Kidd ordered two of *Adventure Galley*'s boats over the side. The men climbed down into them, took bow lines from the ship, and manned their oars. As they pulled at the oars, sweating in the hot sun, *Adventure Galley* began to move again toward her Moorish prize.

Then came a cannon shot.

Just astern of *Adventure Galley*—her sails set so as to work down toward her with the first breath of wind—was a big frigate. As Kidd watched, her guns puffed white smoke again. With the sound of firing came the splash of cannonballs in the water. They fell short of *Adventure Galley* but closer than the first round. Her gunners were getting the range.

Now there was a flutter at the frigate's masthead as her skipper hoisted colors. Even with no wind to make the ensign fly, Captain Kidd could make it out. She was a British warship.

Probably Kidd was not surprised. He knew that the Royal Navy frequently sailed in convoy with the Mocha fleets to help protect the interests of the East India Company. And even though England and France were at war, British navy captains ignored the

French cargoes that were often carried by the Moorish vessels.

So far this warship was not making any progress toward *Adventure Galley*—not while Kidd's men kept to their oars. With this new threat, they worked even harder. Little by little the gap between *Adventure Galley* and the warship lengthened and the distance to the Moorish vessel closed. But Kidd realized that he did not have much time before the frigate could put out her own boats, or a breeze would come up, or those gunners would find his range. He studied the distance to the Moorish ship. His guns might make it. He ordered his gunners to fire.

First he gave the Moor a warning shot. If she struck her colors and backed her sails, he might get a boat aboard her before the warship could come up. But the Moor gave no sign of surrender. So Kidd let her have a broadside.

The first volley was low. Some balls struck the Moorish hull, but most of them splashed into the water short of her. The next round was higher, slashing holes in her sails and cutting her rigging. One of her yardarms came crashing down.

Kidd ordered his gunners to pause. Still she gave no sign. He looked back at the British frigate. She was putting out her boats. Shortly she would be coming down on him, guns firing as she came. Then one of his men pointed ahead of the Moorish ship. Another big vessel was swinging slowly about to head for them. Her gun ports were opening as she turned. Off to the west a slight breeze was beginning to disturb the waters of the gulf. Already it was lifting the colors of the second vessel so Kidd could see that she was a Dutch warship, also helping protect the convoy.

It was too late. If *Adventure Galley* stayed any longer, she would be surrounded by British and Dutch warships. And since she had fired on her intended prize, the warships would not stop for their commanders to ask questions. They would blow *Adventure Galley* out of the water.

So, while the men in the boats strained even harder at their oars, Captain Kidd turned *Adventure Galley* away from the Mocha fleet.

The British frigate kept firing at her as she ran for the cover of the islands. But as she moved off, both warships stayed with the convoy, and *Adventure Galley* escaped. As they moved away, Captain Kidd could hear the men on the deck below cursing their luck—and him.

Adventure Galley's luck, it turned out, was even worse than her men realized. The British frigate was H.M.S. *Sceptre,* and her captain, Edward Barlow, had got close enough to identify *Adventure Galley*. When the Mocha fleet reached India, a letter went off to London. *Adventure Galley*, it reported, had attacked the Mocha fleet. That must mean, the report pointed out, that Captain Kidd had given up pirate-chasing and had turned pirate himself.

The frustrating battle off the Babs was in mid-August of 1697. Kidd now set his course east by north, for India's Malabar Coast. And it was three weeks before they sighted another possible prize.

She was another Moorish ship. *Adventure Galley* sailed alongside her and she quickly hove to. She was no pirate and she carried no French papers. But this time Kidd took a bale of pepper from her and forced two of her men to join his crew, to help navigate in these strange waters. Then he let the Moorish ship go on her way, the rest of her cargo untouched. Even so, he must have realized that he was now coming very close to actual piracy.

By the end of September *Adventure Galley* had reached Carawar, near Goa, on the west coast of India. Kidd went in for water and provisions, and was warned that there were two Portuguese warships patrolling the coast. They seemed to be looking for trouble. Goa was Portugal's colony in India, and Portugal's warships jealously defended the seas nearby. Kidd would be wise to keep away from them. He put to sea and set a watch for them. Next morning, at dawn, the watch hailed below. There they were.

They were huge men-of-war, and they came sweeping down on *Adventure Galley*. Knowing he could not escape, Kidd backed his mainsail and waited for them. As the first warship came alongside, an officer with a speaking trumpet hailed him. What ship and where from? Kidd replied that they were *Adventure Galley* out of London. Where were the warships bound? "Goa," the officer shouted.

Kidd was relieved to see the warships bear off toward the coast. Apparently *Adventure Galley* did not interest them.

Yet, as the day wore on, the warships were still in sight. Instead of continuing on their own course, they seemed to be following *Adventure Galley*. When the sun sank into the sea, the puzzled men of *Adventure Galley* watched the two Portuguese hovering on the horizon, and wondered what they were up to.

By dawn of the next day they knew. In the first light the Portuguese men-of-war could be seen moving into range. The wind was light, and they seemed to be having difficulty closing the distance. But one of them finally came within range. And without any warning, she opened fire.

Adventure Galley rocked under the blow. So devastating was the broadside that some of the cannonballs went through her side and swept her deck. Huge splinters flew through the air. Smoke and dust set everyone coughing. Above the noise of the crunching wood and shouting men came the screams of the wounded. In that first fusillade four of *Adventure Galley*'s men died.

The Portuguese fired again. Now *Adventure Galley*'s gunners were rallying their crews. Kidd gave the command. His gunners returned the fire.

The battle went on all day—hour after hour, with the ships gliding in and out of range and the guns thundering and answering. In the near-calm, the second of the Portuguese ships never got within range. It was fortunate for *Adventure Galley* that she could not, because the first Portuguese did damage enough. By late afternoon eleven of *Adventure Galley*'s men were dead and dozens more were wounded. *Adventure Galley* was badly hurt too, her hull pierced by cannonballs and her sails and rigging torn. But her gun crews were still firing. And now her attacker started to retreat.

The Portuguese looked like a defeated ship. To some of *Adventure Galley*'s men this seemed like the opportunity to go after her and win the fruits of their daylong battle. She was no pirate. She was no Frenchman. But they had not attacked her—she had attacked them. She was a logical prize of war.

Captain Kidd refused. Not only was she not a legal prize, but also there was no certainty that *Adventure Galley*, in her own shattered condition, could catch her anyway. Even if she did, there was that unharmed second Portuguese man-of-war standing by. If *Adventure Galley* chased after her attacker, they could expect her to flee to the protection of her companion. *Adventure Galley*'s crew would do better to spend their time repairing her damage and burying her dead at sea. He set a course away from the Portuguese.

It was nearly a month later, and *Adventure Galley* was still cruising down the Indian coast, when another sail appeared on the horizon. Kidd sent *Adventure Galley* after her and quickly closed on her.

But she did not look promising. She flew British colors. There was little chance that she was a disguised pirate, and even less possibility that she was a Frenchman under false colors. Still, watching the faces of his crew as they watched him, Kidd decided that he had better have a look at the ship's papers anyway.

His boat rowed him across to the ship. As they slid under her counter, he could read her name: *Loyal Captain*. As he climbed aboard, her skipper was waiting for him.

His name was How. *Loyal Captain* was bound from Madras to Surat, with a mixed cargo. Captain Kidd explained that he was patrolling for pirates and Frenchmen, and asked to see *Loyal Captain*'s papers. The papers looked authentically British. Captain Kidd thanked Captain How and apologized for the inconvenience. How and his officers looked relieved. Kidd walked to the rail and climbed down into his boat. But as he lowered himself over the ship's side, he noticed two of his boat crew in conversation with two of the passengers on *Loyal Captain*'s deck.

During the ride back to *Adventure Galley* the rowers said nothing. But Captain Kidd did not like their expressions. Something had excited them. He had not been back aboard his ship for long before he found out.

He gave the order to fill sail and set off again along the coast. But most of his crew were gathered in a circle, talking and pointing toward *Loyal Captain*. Now some of them went below. Before he could send an officer after them, they were back. They came toward his quarterdeck in a group. And they carried pistols.

One crewman stepped forward from the rest. Kidd recognized him. He was William Moore, one of the gunners. Moore started to talk. As he spoke, Captain Kidd knew that he was finally confronted with mutiny.

7

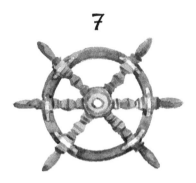

A Mutinous Crew

William Moore faced Captain Kidd and announced that the crew had decided to go over and take that ship before she got away. The men from the boat, he said, had talked to two Dutch passengers who had told them that there were some Greek and Armenian passengers hiding aboard *Loyal Captain*. They were hiding because they carried chests of jewels with them.

Adventure Galley had been at sea for more than a year with nothing to show for it except a small cache of gold and a bale of pepper. So *Adventure Galley*'s men had now voted to return to that ship and seize those chests of jewels. They were going to do it, Moore said, whether Captain Kidd let them or not.

Kidd studied the knot of men gathered around their ringleader. There was no doubt about their intention or their determination. They amounted to two-thirds of his entire crew. Only a few others hung back in the forward part of the ship, warily watching as their shipmates confronted the captain.

Captain Kidd knew he was outnumbered. And the mutineers had armed themselves with pistols stolen from the ship's armory. He knew he could not stop them by force. He turned and looked across at *Loyal Captain*. Her sails were filled but she was not far away. She was moving slowly and in no hurry. *Adventure Galley* had caught her easily a couple of hours ago, and she could do it again. He turned back to his mutinous crew and decided on a gamble.

Kidd told William Moore and his followers that he realized there was no way of stopping them if they were determined to do what they threatened. But if they did, he reminded them, they were no longer privateers. They were pirates.

William Moore interrupted. He had a plan. They would not only take the ship, but they would also force her captain to sign a statement saying that some other ship—not *Adventure Galley*—had been his captor.

That, Captain Kidd replied, "is a Judas trick." And it would not work anyway.

Moore responded that beggars could not be choosers, and "we are beggars already."

They were more than beggars, Captain Kidd told them. They were mutineers. And now they were planning to become pirates. Then he tried his gamble.

If anyone from *Adventure Galley* went over to take that ship, he announced, they were no longer members of his crew. They would not be permitted to return to *Adventure Galley*. Furthermore, he would treat them as the pirates and mutineers they were. He and the rest of his crew would attack *Loyal Captain,* seize her and his rebellious men, take them into Bombay, and hand them over to the British authorities in that port. He hoped that everyone knew what the British government did to pirates.

He studied the faces of the men as they listened to him. A few seemed to waver. Then someone pulled William Moore back, and a circle formed again while the men talked and argued among themselves.

Kidd stood and watched them. Would they call his bluff? He knew, and they knew, that he had no chance of defeating and capturing them—if enough of them joined the mutineers and went over to the other ship. But would enough of them take the chance? And could enough of them get aboard *Loyal Captain* in *Adventure Galley*'s boats to surprise and subdue her crew? Would his men decide instead to lock him up, seize *Adventure Galley,* and use her to capture the other vessel? That would mean giving up all pretense to being privateers, and all hope of returning to their homes except as hunted men. Would they decide to go that far?

One by one the men began to drift back out of the circle. The group remaining and arguing with each other grew smaller and smaller. Kidd saw that he was winning. Within a few minutes the last of the mutineers gave up in disgust.

Kidd immediately had an officer collect the pistols and lock them up. He decided not to confine or lash any of the men. He needed them to work the ship and to fight any future battle like the one he had fought against the Portuguese. He even let Gunner Moore go without punishment. He hoped that Moore and his followers had learned a lesson.

But Kidd must have realized that his men would wonder why he did nothing. They knew all too well how seamen were handled in the Royal Navy. The least sign of disobedience was handled quickly, brutally, and often fatally.

For a minor offense a British seaman was hung by his wrists against a mast and lashed with the infamous "cat," the cat-o'-nine-tails with its nine knotted thongs which cut a man's bare back into a bleeding pulp with only a few strokes. When the victim fainted from the pain, a bucket of salt water dashed into the open wounds revived him, screaming with agony. For worse infractions a man could be "keel hauled." Tied to two ropes, he was tossed overboard at the bow and dragged underwater the length of the ship, its barnacles gashing him as he fought to keep from drowning.

If anything approaching *Adventure Galley*'s mutinous outbreak occurred aboard a navy ship, the ring leaders were "flogged through the fleet." Rowed from ship to ship, they were strung up and lashed aboard each one, so the entire fleet could witness the punishment and learn a lesson from it. Often the mutineers were unconscious by the time they were hoisted aboard the last ship. But still their bleeding bodies were strung up and a new flogging lashed into the pulpy flesh. Frequently a victim did not survive a flogging through the fleet.

But *Adventure Galley* was not a navy ship. William Kidd was a privateer, not an admiral. And he decided not to punish his men, despite the provocation.

Two weeks later *Adventure Galley* was running before a soft wind. The sky was cloudless. The rhythmic creak of the masts and steady wash of the sea alongside had put many of the off-watch crew to sleep. Captain Kidd was below in his cabin. But if he was napping, he was awake enough to notice the mumbling conversation on deck, and to realize that it was becoming louder. As he listened, he recognized the loudest voice. It was that of Gunner Moore.

Kidd went on deck to see what it was all about. He found Moore at the ship's grindstone, pedaling it and holding a chisel against the whirring sandstone wheel. Sparks flew and the blade of the chisel sang as its edge was sharpened by the wheel.

Moore saw the captain and paused. The grindstone wheel slowly spun to a stop.

Kidd asked what the arguing was about.

Moore replied that everyone was complaining, as usual, about their bad luck. But he wasn't calling it luck. He knew better. They had seen enough prizes to make them rich many times over. But the captain would not let them take advantage of their good fortune when it was right in front of them. No, it wasn't bad luck, Moore grumbled. It was a captain who was deliberately doing them out of their shares.

Captain Kidd looked at the men around Moore. It seemed like a replay of the scene two weeks earlier. He looked out to sea and there he saw the reason.

She was a big ship, and she was almost within range. They were near enough so Kidd could make out her colors. They were Dutch.

Of course she might carry a French pass. But Kidd knew that this time he had better not board her to find out. If he ever got a boat's crew aboard that ship, with his men in the mood they were, the Dutch ship would become a prize—legally or not.

Gunner Moore was almost shouting now. They should never have let *Loyal Captain* escape, he said. That one ship would have made all of them rich. His followers nodded. Moore pointed the chisel at Captain Kidd and cried: "You ruin us!"

That did it. Kidd knew now that he had made a major mistake not to put this mutineer in irons two weeks ago. It might now be too late. Moore was inciting the rest of the crew all over again. Kidd would have to act fast to assert his authority. Otherwise the men would not only attack the Dutchman, they might also seize *Adventure Galley* from him.

He could no longer simply order the men to take Moore below and put him in irons. It was too late for that. The men were on Moore's side, not the captain's. Kidd dared not seize Moore himself. He might find himself grabbed by Moore's followers.

But he had to act, and he had to do it immediately. Kidd had no weapon, while Moore still held that heavy, sharpened chisel in his hand. At that moment Kidd noticed the water bucket.

It was wooden, bound with brass hoops. It was heavy but maneuverable, with a sturdy handle. It was hardly the perfect weapon. But it was the only one at hand.

With one sweeping motion Captain Kidd stooped, snatched up the bucket by the handle, and swung it. In a flashing arc it smacked into the side of William Moore's head. Moore never had time to duck.

The only sounds were the smack of the bucket as it struck Moore's head, and the thump and clatter as Moore fell and the chisel dropped onto the deck.

The crew stood looking on, startled into immobility. Before they could recover, Kidd gave the order to take Moore below. Two men gathered up the unconscious body and shuffled off to carry it down the steep companionway to the row of hammocks which served as *Adventure Galley*'s sick bay.

Captain Kidd ordered the rest of the crew back to their stations. *Adventure Galley* stayed on her course. The unknown Dutchman, now safe from attack, disappeared over the horizon.

Next day the doctor brought the news to Captain Kidd: William Moore was dead.

THE GREAT PRIZE

The death of William Moore was a turning point. Now *Adventure Galley*'s luck suddenly changed.

It was just after sunset on November 18, 1697, when the lookout called down to report some running lights on the horizon. There was no way of telling what sort of ship it might be, or of what nationality. But dawn would tell. Captain Kidd sent *Adventure Galley* after her.

Through the night they followed the stranger's lights, keeping their own ship in darkness. It was difficult to tell whether they were gaining on her. But at least the lights never disappeared. Then as the sky in the east began to grow light, the lights slowly dimmed.

There, in the first glimmer of dawn, were her sails. The ship was closer than her lights had seemed. Studying her through the glass. Captain Kidd ordered all sails set to run down on her. Unless he was mistaken at this distance, she was flying a French flag.

He was not mistaken. As they drew closer he could make out her flag flying in the light breeze. To lure her captain into the trap, Kidd ordered a French flag hoisted on *Adventure Galley*.

By mid-morning they were within hailing distance. At the sight of the French flag the stranger had slowed to wait for him. Kidd sent for a crewman named LeRoy, and told him to hail the ship in French.

The ship sat in the water a few hundred yards away from them, her sails slatting as she rolled with the swells. Her boat was lowered and started toward them. The ship looked a bit smaller than *Adventure Galley*, perhaps about two hundred tons. She had a few gun ports, but they were still closed. Evidently the ruse had worked. In any case, she did not look like a match for *Adventure Galley* in a fight.

The boat came alongside. Kidd asked LeRoy to pose as captain of *Adventure Galley*. He would keep up the pretense of being French for a while longer.

The stranger's captain climbed on deck, followed by a dozen attendants. He was a Mohammedan, but he spoke French. LeRoy responded in French and invited the visitors into the captain's cabin. Kidd went along, pretending to be first mate.

In *Adventure Galley*'s cabin the visiting captain obligingly presented his papers. They included a French pass, issued by the French East India Company to grant the ship safe passage past any patrolling French warships.

Captain Kidd stepped forward, identified himself, and took the French pass.

Here at last, after almost two years, was the first big prize of the expedition. Her name was *Rouparelle,* and she was carrying a cargo of silks, jewels, and coin worth £5,000 (nearly a million dollars by today's values[1]).

There was a celebration aboard *Adventure Galley* that night. Every jewel, doubloon, and piece of eight was divided into shares, with sixty percent for the crew as promised in New York. The men lined up on deck to receive their shares. One by one they came up to the table set on deck and each man swept his loot into his hat or cap. There was no way to spend any of it out here in the Indian Ocean. But the thought of their reward, at long last, was enough to set off a wild party.

Next morning Captain Kidd sent a prize crew aboard *Rouparelle* and set a course for Madagascar. He

---

1. Bank of England inflation calculator for the years 1697-2020

was worried about the condition of *Adventure Galley*. Her hull was caked with barnacles and festooned with weed, and the teredo worm had bored so deeply into her planks that she was leaking constantly. It was time for careening again, and Madagascar seemed a safe place for it.

Also, Madagascar was on the way home. If they found no more prizes in the next few weeks, it might be a good idea to return to New York. What was left of *Rouparelle*'s cargo after the share-out must be worth more than £2,000 ($375,000 by today's values[1]). The syndicate had invested a little less than that in the entire expedition. So already they should be getting their money back.

Kidd knew that he had not followed the letter of the law. His commission instructed him to wait until *Adventure Galley* returned to America before sharing out any treasure. But he also knew that if he had tried to hold back the crew's share after all this time, he would have had another mutiny on his hands. In any case, he felt sure that he could explain everything on his return now that his luck had turned. To be sure, he had found no pirates. But at least he had something to show for the expedition.

The winds were light, and *Adventure Galley* and her prize drifted slowly southward. They also drifted

---

1. Bank of England

apart. But Kidd didn't worry. He was sure that the prize crew was as anxious to reach Madagascar and prepare for the last leg home as he was.

Still he kept on the lookout for any more ships—either pirate or Frenchman. And two months later, while he was still drifting down the Indian coast, he came upon the biggest prize of all.

She was a huge merchantman, of at least four hundred tons. She was nearly twice the size of *Adventure Galley,* but she evidently carried only ten guns. *Adventure Galley* carried thirty. They bore down on her about ten miles off the Cochin coast. Even at a distance, Kidd could see that if the vessel carried a French pass, he would really strike it rich.

He ordered the French flag hoisted again.

The big merchantman did not answer *Adventure Galley*'s signal, but kept plowing straight ahead. She was sluggish, though, and *Adventure Galley* slowly caught up with her. At a hailed command the merchantman's skipper backed her mainsail and put a boat over the side. While Kidd and his crew watched, gunners at their station in case of ambush, the boat slid over to *Adventure Galley.* Two men climbed aboard and presented themselves. One was the captain and one the gunner.

As they introduced themselves. Captain Kidd turned

to his mate and ordered *Adventure Galley*'s colors changed. The French flag came down and the British ensign went up.

The merchantman's captain gasped. "You are English?"

Kidd said yes.

"Which is the captain?"

Kidd replied that he was.

The captain handed him his papers and said, "Here is a good prize." Kidd opened them and found another French pass.

Her name was *Quedagh Merchant,* and she made *Rouparelle* look like a lumber schooner. *Quedagh Merchant*'s hold was a treasure trove: silks and muslins, calico and opium, and thousands upon thousands of pieces of "Arab gold." At a quick calculation her cargo appeared to be worth more than £10,000, or nearly two million dollars by present values.[1] This was a prize indeed, one worth the expedition many times over. And not a shot had been fired.

Captain Kidd was in a much greater hurry to reach Madagascar now. He had sent the crews of *Rouparelle* and *Quedagh Merchant* ashore in their own boats. So he was using nearly all his own crew in manning the two prizes. He realized that if he ran across another potential victim, he would not have enough men to be

1. Bank of England

able to attack. If he encountered a warship like those Portuguese, things would be even worse.

Moreover, by now *Adventure Galley* was leaking so badly that they had to run cables under her bottom and up her sides, drawing them tight to keep her hull from falling apart. Meanwhile the men worked day and night to pump out the water that steadily leaked into her hold.

So it was an exhausted crew that finally sighted St. Mary, on the eastern shore of Madagascar, on April 1, 1698. *Adventure Galley* limped into the harbor with *Quedagh Merchant* in her wake. *Rouparelle* followed shortly.

And there, at long last, was a pirate.

When Captain Kidd discovered who the pirate was, he must have felt a secret delight. It was Robert Culliford, the same man who many years earlier had persuaded the crew to seize Kidd's trading schooner in the West Indies. Now, in the harbor of St. Mary, Kidd was told that the ship lying at anchor, within gunshot, was commanded by "Captain" Culliford. Here was his opportunity for revenge.

But he did not get his revenge after all.

Perhaps the sight of the rich loot had only made his men greedier than ever. Perhaps most of them were pirates at heart, and had been all along. Whatever the reason, most of Kidd's crew went over the side into *Adventure Galley*'s boats and rowed over to join "Captain" Culliford.

Kidd was left with hardly enough men to work one ship. Even if he had had a full crew, he could hardly have sailed *Adventure Galley,* in her rotted condition, down around the Cape of Good Hope and across the Atlantic Ocean. So he transferred everything aboard *Quedagh Merchant.* And he waited for the changing season to bring a trade wind that would take him down to the Cape.

He waited for months, all through the summer while the trade winds blew against him. While he waited, he watched his former crewmen burn and scuttle *Rouparelle* and what was left of *Adventure Galley.* At one point Kidd had to barricade himself in *Quedagh Merchant*'s cabin. The rebels left him alone, but they got away with part of *Quedagh Merchant*'s cargo. They also stole his journal and burned it. Then, in Culliford's ship, they sailed out of the harbor and headed north, running before the wind.

Kidd realized that they were going pirating and that he could do nothing to stop them. Here he was, the captain sent out to capture pirates, watching his first pirate sail away from him, with his own crew. He could only wait for the prevailing winds to change. When finally they did, he set out for home.

It was a long, rough crossing and his ship was undermanned. Kidd took *Quedagh Merchant* down around the southern point of Madagascar and along the coast of Africa to the Cape of Good Hope. Rounding the Cape, he set the course for the long straight run northwest to the West Indies, North America, and home. It was the longest leg of the voyage, more than five thousand miles. Storms swept over them as they approached the equator. Night after night the men were called on deck to reef sail, while the winds tried to blow them off the yardarms and the ship heeled so that at one moment they were almost in the sea and the next moment they were swinging high over the deck. *Quedagh Merchant*'s men were exhausted by the time they reached the West Indies. It was April of 1699, five months after their departure from Madagascar, when the lookout called down that he could see land.

Anguilla, set among the British West Indies, was a quiet tropical island. *Quedagh Merchant*'s anchor went down in water so clear that the men could see it touch bottom. The trade winds crooned in the rigging. Tall palm trees seemed to wave to them from the beach. Captain Kidd ordered a boat over the side, climbed down, and went ashore to gather provisions, fresh water, and whatever news there might be.

There was, indeed, news. Captain Kidd had been proclaimed a pirate. There was a price on his head, and a naval fleet had been sent out to get him.

This is what had happened. While *Adventure Galley* had been cruising the Indian Ocean, one report after another had come into London accusing Captain Kidd of piracy. Captain Barlow of H.M.S. *Sceptre* had complained that *Adventure Galley* had attacked the Mocha fleet near the Babs. The skipper of the Moorish vessel, from which Kidd had taken the bale of pepper and the two men to help him navigate, had made a formal protest. So had the owners of *Rouparelle* and *Quedagh Merchant,* neglecting to mention that their ships carried French passes.

As these reports came into London, the members of *Adventure Galley*'s syndicate began to fear that they had been double-crossed. If the reports were to be believed, the man they had sent pirate-chasing had become a pirate himself. As his partners they could be accused of piracy too—unless they could make him their scapegoat.

They chose a roundabout way of doing it. Every few years the British government used an ingenious device for reducing the number of pirates on the high seas. The Crown proclaimed an amnesty, or pardon, for any pirates who would give themselves up and return to an honest life. The amnesty worked well. Frequently there were many pirate crews who were ready to give up if only they could escape the hangman's noose. They were weary of being forever on the run. They were homesick. And often they were as rich as they had ever wanted to be, but could not return home to enjoy their loot. So they waited for the proclamation of amnesty, came home, and "took the King's pardon," as they called it.

But this time the King proclaimed an amnesty with a difference. This time any pirate would be granted a pardon, with two exceptions—Captain Henry Every, whom Captain Kidd had gone out to find, and Captain Kidd himself.

In addition a small fleet was sent out to the Indian Ocean to capture Kidd. The members of the syndicate did not want to take the chance of having him surrender and expose them. It would be safer to bring him in, jail him, try him quickly and quietly, and get it over with. So the fleet was sent out after him with orders to bring him back to London, dead or alive.

Somewhere near the Cape of Good Hope, Captain Kidd and *Quedagh Merchant* unknowingly passed his pursuers. So Kidd sailed all the way to Anguilla, on the other side of the Atlantic, before he discovered that officially he was a pirate.

Anguilla was a British island. Captain Kidd could not expect any help in getting provisions here. He was lucky to slip away without being captured. Up came *Quedagh Merchant*'s anchor, and Kidd sailed off to St. Thomas.

At the time St. Thomas belonged to Denmark. Kidd hoped that the Danish governor of the island, even if he knew of the British proclamation, would permit Kidd to buy enough food for the rest of the voyage. He was sure that if he could get to New York, Lord Bellomont would protect him. Bellomont had by now taken up his office as governor of New York and New England. It had been Bellomont who had "persuaded" Kidd to go on this expedition in the first place. If he could get to New York and explain everything to Bellomont, Kidd was sure that he would be all right.

Kidd decided against sailing into the harbor of St. Thomas. He could not be sure of the reception he would receive. If the governor of the island tried to arrest him, he wanted to be outside the harbor and ready to make a run for it. So Kidd sailed up to the harbor entrance and sent a boat into town, while he waited outside to see what would happen.

The governor of St. Thomas, John Lorentz, had already heard the news that a William Kidd had been proclaimed a pirate. And here was an officer representing the same William Kidd and asking for permission to purchase supplies for a voyage to New York. Governor Lorentz called a meeting of his council. What should they do?

St. Thomas was a Danish island surrounded by British islands. The governor of St. Thomas was not required to honor the British request to capture Captain Kidd. But St. Thomas traded back and forth with the British islands and depended on this trade for its survival. Governor Lorentz and his council decided not to take any chances. They should not help Captain Kidd. In fact, they decided to alert the British.

Two messages went out. One informed Captain Kidd that he would not be permitted to land. The second message went to the governor of British Barbados, notifying him that Captain Kidd had turned up at St. Thomas. If they wanted him, they had better come and get him. The governor of Barbados acted immediately. The British warship *Queensborough* was sent north to St. Thomas with orders to capture the pirate, Captain Kidd.

By the time *Queensborough* arrived off St. Thomas, *Quedagh Merchant* had disappeared. Captain Kidd took her to the island of Curaçao, which he remembered from his earlier voyages to the West Indies. Here he found an old friend. Henry Bolton had been the collector of customs at Antigua. Now he was a merchant. And he happened to have a ship he was prepared to sell. She was the sloop *St. Anthony.* The more Captain Kidd thought about it, the more he felt that a sloop like *St. Anthony* was a better vessel for the last leg to New York than the battered and leaky *Quedagh Merchant* after her long transatlantic crossing.

So he bought the sloop from his friend. Before setting off for New York, Kidd convoyed *Quedagh Merchant* to a safe hiding place. At the island of Hispaniola he anchored her in a bay in the Higüey River. With an anchor at her stern and her bow tied to the trees, he left her to await his return. Kidd then headed north for New York.

But first he took one more precaution. From Curaçao he sent a message to a friend in New York. James Emmot, he remembered, was one of the best lawyers in the city. Emmot could tell him what sort of reception he would receive, and whether it was safe for him to sail into New York harbor. So Kidd asked Emmot if they could meet in Oyster Bay, in Long Island Sound, before *St. Anthony* went the last few miles into New York.

The message reached Emmot in time, and he was waiting when Kidd took *St. Anthony* into the east entrance to Long Island Sound and along the sound to Oyster Bay. *St. Anthony*'s anchor was hardly down when a boat came out from the shore. Watching from his deck, Captain Kidd saw that not only his friend Emmot had come to meet him. So had Sarah and Elizabeth.

9

Buried Treasure

Captain Kidd's wife and daughter had not seen him for nearly three years. They too had heard that he had been declared a pirate. Almost certainly they refused to believe this proclamation. He was Sarah's husband and Elizabeth's father. That was all that mattered to them.

To Sarah, William Kidd looked worn and thin and a little older. To him Sarah looked unchanged. But Elizabeth had grown from a baby to a young girl, a five-year-old who now looked at him with curiosity. She had scarcely known him as her father when he had set sail from New York that morning in September of

1696. And whatever she knew of him then she had forgotten in his absence.

Now she looked up at the tall figure standing on the deck and let him scoop her up and kiss her. Then she looked around at what amazed her much more—the soaring mast of the sloop, the water all around them, and the bewildering tangle of lines running in every direction.

For the first few minutes Captain Kidd devoted himself to the reunion with his wife and daughter. Then he realized that he must get back to business. Turning to Emmot, he asked the questions that had been worrying him since he had left Anguilla.

Was it really true that he was officially declared a pirate? Why? What had happened to the syndicate? Were they betraying him?

James Emmot answered as briefly as possible. There was a lot to explain. His Excellency Lord Bellomont had come to New York some time ago, shortly after *Adventure Galley* had left on her voyage. Bellomont had announced that he was going to change things in New York. There would be no more business with pirates. Smugglers would be tracked down and prosecuted. Lord Bellomont was going to reform New York. And all the merchants and politicians who had done business with pirates and smugglers had better take warning.

Captain Kidd must have smiled to himself as he heard this. Here was Lord Bellomont, founder of a conspiracy to make money out of pirate-chasing, pretending to be the reformer of sinful New York. But after all, Bellomont was the man who had forced Captain Kidd into his present situation. Surely Bellomont was the man who would get him out of it.

Captain Kidd had no way of knowing what had led the King to proclaim him as a pirate. But Bellomont had the King's ear. Perhaps he had been unable to say anything at the time, since Kidd had been halfway around the world, and Bellomont had no way to find out Kidd's side of the affair.

But now he did. All Captain Kidd had to do was sit down with Lord Bellomont and tell him the whole story. Time after time he had turned away from an easy prize because it was neither a pirate nor a Frenchman. He had even faced down a mutiny because of his refusal to turn pirate. He could not imagine what had led to the proclamation, but he guessed that word of his two captures had reached London. There had been time enough for this while Kidd had sat out the contrary winds at Madagascar and then fought his way around the Cape and up the Atlantic. But even if no one in London knew of the French passes which made his captures legal, Captain Kidd knew. And he had the passes to prove it.

Where, he asked Emmot, was Lord Bellomont?

Emmot explained that Lord Bellomont was not in New York. He had moved to Boston. Evidently His Excellency had decided that New York had been fairly well cleaned up, and it was time to go to work on Boston. In any case, Captain Kidd must go there if he wished to see Bellomont.

But first Emmot offered some words of warning. Captain Kidd should be prepared to find a changed Lord Bellomont. For one thing, there were rumors in New York that politics had entered into the business of the voyage of *Adventure Galley*.

In London the opposition—the Tory Party—was preparing for elections. One way to win an election against the party in power—in fact, just about the most effective way to do it—is to prove that the party in power is corrupt, or has acted deceitfully or secretly. The opposition party in England was beginning to make noises about the now-famous voyage of Captain Kidd. Instead of a pirate-chasing expedition, it had begun to look like a piratical adventure itself. Not only that, but the whole scheme had been arranged by a group of the King's ministers, who expected to make a great deal of money out of the expedition.

So went the accusation of the opposition party in London. And because of this, said Emmot, Captain

Kidd should be extremely careful. Of course he could prove that he had not been a pirate. But it was possible that Lord Bellomont and the rest of the syndicate might not be interested in proving Captain Kidd's innocence.

Why? Because to prove that he had not been a pirate, Captain Kidd would have to describe his entire venture from start to finish. To do that he would have to reveal the existence of the syndicate. All sorts of politically embarrassing questions would then arise. And even if Captain Kidd's innocence were finally established, a hint of corruption would continue to hang over the King's ministers.

So it might be much easier for them simply to announce that a group of ministers had, for patriotic reasons, pooled their funds to send one Captain William Kidd out chasing pirates. Captain Kidd had betrayed them by becoming a pirate himself. Therefore they denounced him and condemned him to death.

This was James Emmot's analysis of the situation. In short, the King's ministers were in a political jam. Someone had to be sacrificed. Captain Kidd was that man.

As he listened to Emmot's warnings, William Kidd probably reminded himself that James Emmot and Lord Bellomont could not possibly have had much friendship or regard for each other. Emmot was a seaman's lawyer. He had defended many a smuggler and even pirate in his time. Certainly Lord Bellomont knew that. If Bellomont were trying to make a name for himself as the scourge of the pirates of New York and New England, the two men had probably clashed. So there was no reason to believe everything James Emmot said about Lord Bellomont.

Still there was no real reason to disbelieve him either. It was quite possible that Lord Bellomont and the rest of the syndicate members were waiting to pounce on Kidd and use him as their scapegoat. That in fact would explain the mystery of why he had already been denounced, before he had even reached home.

Kidd decided on a cautious approach. He asked Emmot if he would go up to Boston and deliver a message to Bellomont. If Emmot made the first contact, Kidd would have a chance to study Bellomont's reaction before deciding whether or not to give himself up.

Emmot agreed to act as his messenger. Kidd sat down and wrote a letter to Lord Bellomont. In it he made two points. First, he was not a pirate. Second, he had brought back enough treasure to provide an excellent return on the syndicate's investment. He had, he added cautiously, left most of the treasure aboard *Quedagh Merchant* at Hispaniola. He would return and retrieve it as soon as his innocence had been established. To prove he was no pirate, Kidd sent Lord Bellomont the two French passes.

The sloop *St. Anthony* put out of Oyster Bay with Emmot and Captain Kidd's wife and daughter aboard. They sailed down Long Island Sound to Stonington, Connecticut, where Emmot went ashore to go overland to Boston. Captain Kidd then took the sloop back to sea, to await Lord Bellomont's answer.

Meanwhile he took another precaution. He expected Bellomont to react favorably to the news that he had brought back so much treasure. If anything would persuade the syndicate members not to betray him, it would be the fact that they would profit from the voyage. But if they were really waiting to make him their scapegoat, they could do it as soon as they had laid hands on the treasure. That was one reason he had mentioned that most of it was still down in the West Indies. And now he did something that has made Captain Kidd famous ever since. He buried some of the treasure.

Off the end of Long Island lies a triangle of sand, forest, and marsh known as Gardiner's Island. Then, as now, it was owned by a member of the Gardiner family, to whom the island had been granted by the Crown many years earlier.

So it was that John Gardiner looked from the window of his house and watched a strange sloop tack into his harbor. In the proper spirit of hospitality, Gardiner went out to the sloop to welcome his visitor.

The name William Kidd meant nothing to him. The visitor seemed pleasant enough. When he asked if he could leave a chest of belongings in a forest behind Gardiner's beach, buried in the sand to protect it from other visitors, Gardiner consented. It would have made more sense to keep the chest in one of the sheds. But Captain Kidd was not the first eccentric visitor Gardiner had welcomed to his island. So he agreed to the odd request, and he even signed the receipt which Captain Kidd presented to him.

When the treasure chest was safely buried, *St. Anthony* moved out of the harbor again. Captain Kidd took her across the sound and into Narragansett Bay to wait for Emmot and the response from Lord Bellomont.

Emmot returned with a letter from Lord Bellomont. The letter assured Kidd of a warm welcome and his lordship's support. "Mr. Emmot delivered me two French passes," Bellomont wrote, "which passes I have in my custody, and I am apt to believe they will be a

good article to justify you...." His lordship went on to say that he had consulted with the proper authorities in London, "and they are of the opinion that if your case be so clear as you (or Mr. Emmot for you) have said, that you may safely come hither, and be equipped and fitted out to go and fetch the other ship."

And then his lordship added what must have been the most persuasive line in his letter. "I make no manner of doubt," he said, "but to obtain the King's pardon for you and those few men you have left, who I understand have been faithful to you and have refused as well as you to dishonor the Commission you had from England."

Was Bellomont trying to trap him? Perhaps. But Kidd had fulfilled his part of the bargain. He had brought back enough treasure to repay the syndicate's investment handsomely. So why shouldn't Bellomont welcome him and help prove his innocence? All they had to do was pay off the members of the syndicate and produce the French passes, and there would be no more question about piracy.

Moreover, to look at it another way, what was the alternative? Run away? Hide out? For how long before they tracked him down? He would then become a pirate in fact, living like an outlaw. Would he ever see his wife and daughter again? And why run? He already had enough treasure from the two captures for himself as well as the syndicate members.

No, he had to trust in the good will of Lord Bellomont. They had made a contract. He had carried out his part of it. He could only trust Lord Bellomont to do the same.

He wrote Bellomont that he would come to Boston. And he added: "I do further declare and protest that I never did in the least act contrary to the King's Commission, nor to the Reputation of my honorable Owners, and doubt not but I shall be able to make my Innocency appear, or else I had no need to come to these parts of the world."

St. Anthony's anchor came up again. And Captain Kidd set the sloop's course around Cape Cod for Boston.

His Excellency Lord Bellomont, governor of New York and New England, was in trouble. He had boasted that he was going to clean up all the smuggling and piracy in this area, but this was turning out to be a lot more difficult than he had thought. It was incredible how many ingenious devices the colonists could use to baffle or corrupt the customs inspectors. And their swift little trading sloops slipped past the British patrols in an almost steady stream. Not only that, but the merchants in New York and Boston were resisting the new governor's cleanup in dozens of devious ways. They falsely labeled goods, forged clearance documents, and hid shipments in warehouses all along the coast. The merchants had made a good business out of smuggling and dealing with pirates, and they did not want to give it up.

Now, on top of everything else, came the matter of Captain Kidd. It could hardly help Bellomont's cleanup campaign if the governor himself were exposed as a backer of a piratical adventure. In fact, it would make him the laughingstock of the colonies.

Bellomont had already received some warning letters from London. The merchants of New York and Boston had complained that his administration was crippling the cities' commerce. Bellomont had replied that these complainers were dealers with pirates and therefore beneath notice. And now he was in danger of being denounced as little better than a pirate himself—the partner of Captain Kidd.

It was all very annoying and frustrating. Besides, the governor was suffering another attack of gout. And his wife, once famous in London as the beautiful "Countess Kate," was behaving no better in Boston than she had in London. She was running up huge debts and flirting with every young man until Lord Bellomont was almost insane with jealousy. So it was no wonder that the Bellomont who greeted Captain Kidd was a very different man from the self-assured new governor whom Kidd had met in London four years earlier.

His lordship kept the captain waiting three days, in fact. Then Kidd was summoned to appear before Bellomont and his council. The governor was obviously in a vile humor. He wasted no time on welcome but proceeded to business. Would Captain Kidd give a full account of his voyage? Where was his journal? His commission had specifically requested a detailed narrative of the expedition. Why had he not produced it?

Captain Kidd explained that he had kept a journal, but that the rebellious crew members had stolen it and burned it at Madagascar. Bellomont demanded a new one. He would give Captain Kidd until 5 P.M. the next day to write it.

Kidd tried, but found that he could not produce an entirely new journal, with all the countless dates and places of every detail of the voyage, in such a short time. He reported to the council next day that he was at work on it but had not completed it. Bellomont reluctantly gave him another day and dismissed him. When Kidd had left the council room, the governor told the council members that he had already received his orders from London. Kidd was to be arrested and sent to London for trial.

Next day Kidd appeared to report that he was nearly finished with the new journal. He found a sheriff waiting for him. And while his backer and "protector" watched, Captain Kidd was led down the steps of the governor's mansion and off to jail.

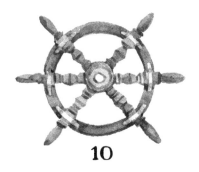

10

TRIAL AND TREACHERY

His Majesty's Ship *Advice* sailed out of New York harbor in February of 1700, bound for London. Aboard were thirty-three "pirates" being sent to England for trial. One of them was William Kidd.

Kidd had reason to remember H.M.S. *Advice*. She had been one of the warships he had encountered near the Cape of Good Hope, on his way out to Madagascar and the Indian Ocean. He had dined in her wardroom with her officers. And now, aboard the same ship, he was confined in a tiny cabin down in steerage, as a prisoner charged with piracy.

But the irony could hardly have amused him. He

had every reason to be despondent. For more than six months he had been in a cell in Boston's old Stone Prison, his wrists and ankles chained to the wall. Sarah and Elizabeth had not been permitted to see him. He had been taken from the prison and rushed to New York under heavy guard, to be herded aboard *Advice*. There were no farewells to his wife and daughter this time. *Advice* quickly put to sea.

In the Thames, as the ship approached London, a special delegation met the "pirates" and whisked them off to jail. Captain Kidd found himself in Britain's most famous prison, Newgate.

At least he could now prepare for the trial. He had finished his narrative of the expedition by now. So he asked for the documents and letters he had sent to Lord Bellomont—particularly the French passes that he felt sure would prove his innocence.

But the weeks turned into months, and still he remained in Newgate prison. At first he was chained to the wall. But later Newgate's warden managed to get permission to unchain him and give him the freedom of his small, damp cell. The warden argued that if the prisoner did not get some exercise, he might not live long enough to stand trial.

Kidd had a long time to wait. It was almost a year before the trial would be held, a year that was spent in maneuvering between the political parties. The Tories, who were out of power, tried to get back into power by accusing the Whigs in the King's government of conspiring in a pirate expedition. The Whigs responded by trying to claim there had been no piracy—or if there had been, to blame it all on William Kidd.

It was March of 1701 before a Parliamentary inquest examined Captain Kidd. Evidently the Tories expected him to help their cause by naming and denouncing the members of the syndicate. Instead he simply claimed that he was innocent. There had been no piracy, he said. The Whigs supported him by producing the French passes, which Bellomont had forwarded to London. The disappointed Tories dismissed him. And Parliament voted for the trial.

Kidd must have been relieved to see the French passes in the inquest. He had tried in vain to get them while in jail, to help him prepare his case. But at least they were in London, so he could call for them during the trial when he made his defense.

He had six more weeks to wait in his prison cell before finally, on May 8, 1701, he was led stumbling and blinking out of Newgate and into the Admiralty Court at Old Bailey.

Before him, as he looked about the courtroom, were six solemn, black-robed justices. To one side sat four lawyers—they were the prosecution. There were no lawyers for the defense.

"William Kidd, hold up thy hand."

He did as directed, and then faced the bar.

"May it please your lordships, I desire you to permit me to have counsel."

Sir Salathiel Lovell, one of the judges, spoke for the court: "What would you have counsel for?"

Kidd explained that all his documents had been taken from him. He had asked for them repeatedly but in vain. He now needed a lawyer to help him with his defense, and some time for the lawyer to prepare the case.

Sir Salathiel replied: "The court sees no reason to put off your trial, therefore you must plead."

The Clerk of Arraigns repeated: "William Kidd, hold up thy hand."

Captain Kidd realized that he was expected to plead his own case against four prosecutors. The only witnesses available to help him were also on trial. And on the side of the prosecution he now recognized two of his former crew members. Both had been among the mutineers at Madagascar.

But then came the worst surprise. Captain Kidd expected to defend himself against the charge of piracy. Now he found that there was an extra charge, and that he was to be tried for that first. It was not piracy at all. It was murder.

Almost not believing what he heard, Captain Kidd listened as the prosecutor for the Crown read the charge: while on a voyage in the Indian Ocean the defendant (William Kidd) had struck one William Moore on the head with a wooden bucket, causing the death of said William Moore.

"My lord," said one of the prosecuting attorneys to the bar, "it will appear to be a most barbarous act to murder a man in this manner; for the man gave him no manner of provocation."

No provocation? Kidd listened in astonishment as his former crew members, Joseph Palmer and Robert Bradinham, testified that Captain Kidd, for no reason at all, had suddenly seized a ship's bucket and hit Moore on the head with it, causing Moore's death. When it was Kidd's turn to cross-examine them, he asked Palmer and Bradinham if there hadn't been a near-mutiny aboard *Adventure Galley* at the time. They denied it.

Kidd asked for the testimony of some other crewmen from *Adventure Galley*. To Abel Owens, one of *Adventure Galley*'s sailors, he put the question: "Was there a mutiny among the men?"

Owens answered: "Yes, and the bigger part was for taking the ship."

Other crewmen agreed that if Kidd had not struck Moore, there would have been a mutiny. The prosecutor then rose to argue that the testimony of these witnesses was suspect, since they too were on trial. The justices agreed.

The jury went out for an hour. When they returned, the Clerk of Arraigns said: "Look upon the prisoner. Is he guilty of the murder whereof he stands indicted, or not guilty?"

The jury foreman answered: "Guilty."

Now came the trial for piracy. In his defense Kidd tried to show that he would never consider becoming a pirate. He was gratified to see a few friends from New York and the West Indies come forward to testify to his honesty and respectability. But if the jury was inclined to believe them, the chief justice destroyed any hope.

When Captain Humphreys of New York, for example, described William Kidd as an upright and respectable citizen, the chief justice interrupted to ask: "How long was this ago?"

Captain Humphreys answered: "Twelve years."

"That," said the chief justice, "was before he turned pirate."

The Admiralty Court paid more attention to the testimony of the Madagascar mutineers. Robert Bradinham and Joseph Palmer had been among these mutineers. Both had joined Culliford and gone pirating. Both had taken advantage of "the King's pardon" and come to London under the amnesty. And both were now making doubly sure their lives would be spared by testifying for the prosecution. Describing one period of the voyage, Palmer said: "We coasted about the coast of Malabar."

Mr. Coniers, one of the prosecuting attorneys, asked: "Did you meet with any boats there?"

Palmer: "Yes, several."

Mr. Coniers: "What did you do with them?"

Palmer: "Captain Kidd robbed and plundered them, and turned them adrift again."

Robert Bradinham's contribution was to accuse Kidd of killing Moore, and to deny Kidd's intentions at the Babs. The prosecution asked Kidd about the incident at the Babs, where Kidd had fired on the Moorish vessel. Kidd replied that he had been looking for any vessel that might carry a French pass.

Bradinham was asked for his testimony. "Did Kidd not lie in wait for any French effects in that fleet?"

Bradinham answered: "No, only for the Moorish fleet."

Kidd listened to testimony like this and finally asked: "Mr. Bradinham, are you not promised your life, to take away mine?"

One of the judges interrupted: "He is not bound to answer that question." Bradinham did not.

Another shock awaited Kidd. During the trial he learned that his old enemy Robert Culliford was "in custody," but only for a short while. Robert Culliford had also taken "the King's pardon," and was now going free. And in the process he helped draw the noose tighter around Kidd's neck. Joseph Palmer testified that when they encountered Culliford at Madagascar, Kidd and Culliford had drunk to each other's health aboard *Quedagh Merchant*. Far from ordering his men to attack Culliford, Kidd had helped him. Palmer swore: "Captain Kidd and Culliford were as great friends as could be."

Palmer was turned over to Kidd for cross-examination. The Solicitor General of the court offered: "Ask him what questions you please."

Kidd answered: "It signifies nothing to ask any questions. A couple of rogues will swear anything."

Solicitor General: "Will you ask him any questions?"

Kidd: "No."

Captain Kidd saw that he had only one last hope in which he could place any confidence—the French passes. The two ships he had captured had carried French passes. Whatever flags they flew, whatever nationality their captains pretended, the French passes identified the two vessels as enemies of His Majesty's government.

Captain Kidd had brought the French passes home with him, realizing that they meant the difference between privateering and piracy. He had given them to Lord Bellomont, who had forwarded them to London. Kidd had seen them at the Parliamentary inquest. Now it was time to bring them out and prove his innocence.

He asked that the French passes be presented as evidence.

The court replied: what French passes?

Captain Kidd listened with shock, and then with a sinking heart, as the prosecution accused him of treachery. Certainly any French passes would prove that the defendant was not guilty. But there were no French passes. If there had been any, there would have been no trial.

Kidd pleaded that indeed there were two French passes. He had given them to Lord Bellomont in Boston. Bellomont had passed them to London. They had been seen by Parliament. Where were they?

He pleaded in vain. The Admiralty had simply hidden the French passes. In final despair, William Kidd realized that his last hope, his only solid evidence, had been taken from him and concealed. He now knew that Bellomont and the syndicate members had betrayed him indeed.

He turned to face the black-robed justices. "I will not trouble the court any more," he said. "For it is folly." He sat down.

The presiding judge instructed the jury: "He has told you he acted pursuant to his commission; but that cannot be, unless he gives you satisfaction that the ship and the goods belonged to the French King, or his subjects, or that the ship had a French pass. Otherwise neither of them will excuse him from being a pirate; for if he takes the goods of friends he is a pirate.... As to the French passes, there is nothing of that appears by any proof; and for aught I can see, none saw them but himself, if there were any."

The jury shuffled out. It was gone for only half an hour. When it returned, the Clerk of Arraigns intoned: "Are you agreed on your verdict? How say you, is he guilty of the piracy whereof he stands indicted, or not guilty?"

The jury foreman said: "Guilty."

The Clerk turned to Kidd. "William Kidd, hold up thy hand. What hast thou to say for thyself why thou shouldst not die according to law?"

Kidd replied: "I have nothing to say, but that I have been sworn against by perjured and wicked people."

The chief justice spoke: "William Kidd, you have been tried by the law of the land, and convicted. And nothing now remains but that sentence be passed according to law. And the sentence of the law is this.

"You shall be taken from the place where you are, and be carried to the place from whence you came, and from thence to the place of execution. And there you will be hanged by your neck until you be dead.

"And the Lord have mercy on your soul."

Exactly two weeks later the grated door to Kidd's cell swung open for him for the last time. He was ushered out of Newgate and into an open cart. Ahead of the cart and waiting for him was the Marshal of the Admiralty in his carriage. After him came the Deputy Marshal, carrying the Admiralty's traditional Silver Oar. Two city marshals also waited, their horses wheeling and stomping. The cart jolted forward. Kidd lost his balance and almost fell.

Slowly the procession moved through the streets toward Execution Dock. A few people lined the walks, hushing as the cart rattled by. But at Execution Dock a huge crowd was waiting. Public hangings, especially pirate hangings, were mass spectacles. Londoners came to be entertained and they brought their children to be educated by the example. As Captain Kidd's cart approached, it was greeted by a mounting chorus of shouts and jeers.

Ahead of him, looming against the sky, was the scaffold. It was a soaring wooden pillar, from which hung a swaying rope. At the rope's end was the hangman's noose with its huge looped knot. The sheriffs cleared a path through the crowd. Captain

Kidd was led to the wooden steps and up onto the platform.

The crowd went silent as the executioner lowered the rope and pulled the big loop over Kidd's head. He could feel the bulky knot against his ear. In the hush he could hear the executioner ask: did he have any last words?

Captain Kidd looked out across the Thames. From where he stood he could see the spot where he had weighed anchor aboard *Adventure Galley* to set out on his voyage. He opened his mouth to say something, but he was too late.

The executioner gave the order. The trap door dropped under him. Kidd heard the crowd roar once more as he plummeted down—and stopped with an agonizing jolt that blotted everything out.

Then, just as suddenly, he was alive again. He found himself on the ground under the scaffold, shaking his head groggily. An executioner's assistant was helping him to his feet. And trailing on the ground in front of him was a frayed end of hemp.

Slowly he realized what had happened. The rope had broken. Was this a reprieve? A chaplain appeared beside him. Kidd half-expected the chaplain to say that here was an act of God, William Kidd *was* innocent, and the Lord had interceded to prove it.

But it was too much to hope for. Instead the chaplain was saying something about the Lord granting him a second chance to repent and confess that he *had* been a pirate.

On shaky feet William Kidd let himself be led back up the steps. No, he said to the chaplain, he could not repent what he had not done; he would not confess what he had not been.

The executioner was knotting a new rope. It slipped over Kidd's head. No one asked him for any last words. William Kidd heard the signal again. He heard the crowd's bloodthirsty roar again. And that was the last he heard. This time the rope did not break.

By tradition the execution took place at low tide. And by tradition William Kidd's lifeless body was left dangling, its legs barely touching the ground. The incoming tide reached the toes, the legs, and washed over the body. The tide went out again, came in over the body again, and went out again. Three times the tide washed over Captain Kidd's body. And then it was cut down.

But Admiralty tradition was not through with Captain Kidd. His body was covered with tar to preserve it. It was trussed in chains. Then it was taken to a point near Tilbury Fort, where the land reached out into the Thames. There Captain Kidd's body was hung in the chains, so every sailor setting out to sea could note what happened to pirates, and take warning.

Three days after the execution, while Captain Kidd's body was still swinging in chains near Tilbury Fort, Joseph Palmer and Robert Bradinham, his former crewmen who had testified against him, were pardoned.

On the same day a ship was dispatched to the Indian Ocean, to speed word to the Great Mogul that Captain Kidd was dead. Perhaps this news would help make up for the fact that London could not yet announce the capture of Henry Every. He was never caught.

Two years later Mrs. Sarah Kidd, widow, married one Christopher Rousby in New York. Her daughter Elizabeth assumed the Rousby name, rather than keep the shameful name of Kidd.

And two centuries later an American historian named Ralph D. Paine, doing research in the British Museum and the Public Records Office in London, came upon the hidden French passes that would have saved Captain Kidd.

11

Pirate or Privateer

After nearly three centuries the question remains: are we right to call Captain Kidd a pirate?

Most of us still do. Not long ago the State of New Jersey, in an advertisement for tourists, claimed that "the pirate Captain Kidd was here." Some years ago a man on Block Island, at the end of Long Island Sound, sold a lot but kept what he called "treasure rights," because he felt sure that Captain Kidd had buried treasure on his island as well as Gardiner's Island. More than twenty treasure-hunting expeditions have tried to dig up a "pirate chest" supposedly buried in a deep well on a Nova Scotia island. Legend says the treasure is worth millions and that it was buried there by Captain Kidd.

The legends persist. Yet Captain Kidd's trial and conviction were certainly unfair. His judges were convinced of his guilt before the trial started. His former shipmates were paid off with their lives in return for testifying against him. And the most important evidence in his defense, the French passes, were purposely hidden. In any British or American court today he would be granted a new trial.

But the trial was not really intended to judge his guilt or innocence. It was intended to provide the spectacle behind which his "partners" could hide. Today we would call it a "rigged" trial. Captain Kidd was sacrificed to save the political fortunes of the King's ministers in the syndicate. And the trick worked. After Kidd's public execution, the political storm died down and the King's ministers went about their business—all except Lord Bellomont, who died of what was called "gout in the stomach" (probably uremic poisoning) in New York just before the trial.

Why then do we still call Captain Kidd a pirate? There *are* some reasons.

For one reason, few historians had much cause to believe William Kidd's plea of innocence. For nearly two centuries it was simply assumed that he was guilty as charged. There was only his own word in his defense, and who could believe a pirate? If he really did find French passes on those ships, where were they?

It was more than two hundred years after the trial before the historian Ralph Paine found the passes. Paine had written a number of books on maritime history and was at work on a new one to be called *The Book of Buried Treasure*. He had long suspected that Captain Kidd was not the arch villain his detractors had claimed. Paine was puzzled by the contrast between Kidd's respectable early life in New York and the sudden spree of piracy in the Indian Ocean. And anyone who reads the transcript of Kidd's trial can see how unfair it was.

Like any historian who has done his research in such musty establishments as the British Museum and the Public Records Office, Paine had to plow through boxes of uncatalogued records, papers, and other documents to find anything connected with piracy or treasure. Locating what you are looking for in such libraries quite often is like finding treasure itself. The treasure Paine stumbled onto was the French pass from *Quedagh Merchant*. He later found the one from *Rouparelle*.

With the publication of Paine's book, in 1911, the proof was out. Captain Kidd had captured two ships carrying merchandise for the enemy. Captain Kidd was a privateer, not a pirate.

But history is difficult to change after more than two hundred years. "Captain Kidd the Pirate" had by now become a legend all over the world. And besides, some historians continued to point out that if Captain Kidd were not technically a pirate, he still was not entirely blameless.

For example, he did attack the Mocha fleet. Was he really looking for a Frenchman in disguise? Or would he have taken any ship he could? And there was the Moorish vessel from which he kidnapped two men to serve as navigators. He also took a bale of pepper from that ship. Wasn't that piracy, however insignificant?

What of the sharing-out of *Rouparelle*'s treasure? Captain Kidd's commission called for him to bring all the prizes into New York. If he could not bring *Rouparelle* across the Atlantic, why did he share out the treasure before returning home? At his trial he answered that his men would not have waited. There would have been a mutiny, successful this time, and the men would have taken the syndicate's share too. Of course he had no way then of knowing that they would mutiny later at Madagascar anyway.

Why did Captain Kidd find no pirates? Was it possible to sail all the way through the Indian Ocean, the Gulf of Aden, and the Arabian Sea without ever finding a pirate when the whole area was supposed to be infested with them? Some naval expeditions had.

Captain Kidd simply said that that was what had happened. But who could believe a pirate?

And when at the very last *Adventure Galley* did come upon the pirate Culliford, why didn't Captain Kidd capture him? Some of his men claimed that he even joined forces with Culliford. Captain Kidd testified that his men deserted him and that he did not have enough manpower to attack Culliford's ship. Furthermore, he said, he did not sail out pirating with Culliford and his deserters, but remained in the harbor of St. Mary waiting for a favorable wind to take him home. But who could believe a pirate?

There were other charges. Other ships' captains reported that Captain Kidd had attacked them though they were neither pirates nor French, and carried no French passes. Captain Kidd claimed that he did not attack any other ships. And it is possible that the prize crew aboard *Rouparelle* did some pirating after they had separated from *Adventure Galley* on their way down to Madagascar. Everyone denied such attacks. But who could believe a pirate?

So the legend of "Captain Kidd the Pirate" grew and spread abroad. And when the French passes were finally uncovered, it was not only too late to save William Kidd's life. It was also too late to save his name.

There is another good reason why the legend has gone on and on. The treasure.

On November 15, 1698, when Captain Kidd set sail for home from Madagascar, he still had about £8,000—worth one and a half million dollars by today's values[1]—in jewels, silks, and coin. Even after paying out the crew's share, Kidd had the syndicate's share locked away aboard *Quedagh Merchant*. Back it came with him, across the Atlantic to the West Indies and to *Quedagh Merchant*'s final anchorage in Hispaniola's Higüey River.

When he sailed north to Long Island Sound and Boston in the sloop *St. Anthony*, Captain Kidd told his lawyer friend Emmot that he had left most of the treasure behind with *Quedagh Merchant*. But had he?

Wouldn't he have considered that an unwise move? After what had happened at Madagascar, did he expect the rest of his crew to sit there aboard *Quedagh Merchant* with all that treasure and faithfully wait for his return?

As soon as Kidd was arrested in Boston, Lord Bellomont sent a ship to Hispaniola to get the rest of the treasure. They sailed up the Higüey River and found a blackened hulk, burned to the water's edge. Evidently Kidd's crew had burned *Quedagh Merchant* and fled in all directions with whatever treasure there was.

1. Bank of England

But how much was there? Perhaps not much. It is fair to assume that Captain Kidd knew this would happen, and that he took most of the treasure north with him. If so, what did he do with it?

He buried a chest on Gardiner's Island. But after his arrest, it was quickly recovered, and it contained only a small portion of what had been taken from *Rouparelle* and *Quedagh Merchant*.

He might have given most of it to his wife. But there is nothing about the way she lived thereafter to suggest that she had become so wealthy.

He might have sold it to any of the merchants along Long Island Sound. Again there is nothing to indicate that William Kidd was suddenly a very rich man.

He might have buried it, or at least hidden it. And he could have hidden it in any number of places.

His first port of call as he sailed north was Lewes, on the coast of Delaware. Very little is known about what he did at this stop, besides buying some provisions and getting fresh water. Did he also hide some or all of the syndicate's treasure somewhere on a Delaware beach? Treasure hunters have looked for it for years, in vain.

He could have hidden or buried it somewhere along Long Island Sound. There is a legend among the old-timers on the Thimble Islands, in the sound off New Haven, that Captain Kidd visited these islands. While waiting for Bellomont's reply to his letter, the story goes, Captain Kidd anchored his sloop off one of the Thimbles. He sent a boat ashore and hid a large amount of treasure. Even today one of the Thimbles is called Money Island because of this legend. But Money Island today is a mass of summer cottages. And the island itself is almost solid rock. They say that the treasure was secreted in a cave on the southeast shore of the island. If so, there is no trace of it there now.

He could also have hidden the treasure somewhere in Narragansett Bay. The people around Newport, Rhode Island, still tell stories of the strange goings and comings around Newport right after Captain Kidd had called at Gardiner's Island. And one Newporter at the time claimed that he had dickered with Kidd over hiding some treasure for him. But none of it was ever found.

During his last dark and discouraging days in Newgate prison, Captain Kidd wrote to Lord Bellomont with a proposition. The treasure, he said, was still down on the island of Hispaniola. If he were released from prison, he could lead Lord Bellomont to it.

But Lord Bellomont was sick and dying. No deal was made. Was William Kidd telling the truth? Had he really hidden the treasure there before starting north? Or was this a last-ditch attempt to save his life? No one knows.

No one will ever know, unless some day—on some beach or in some cave along the coast of Hispaniola (now Haiti and the Dominican Republic) or New England—someone comes upon the treasure. Until then the secret of the treasure will remain the biggest mystery of the mysterious voyage of Captain Kidd.

Author's Note

For readers who would like to know more about Captain Kidd, there are two very good books about him. One is The *Fateful Voyage of Captain Kidd* by Dunbar Maury Hinrichs, and the other is *Pirate Laureate* by William Hallam Bonner. These books may not be easy to find, but your local librarian may be able to borrow them from another library.

If you wish to read more about piracy, you might like my book *Famous Pirates of the New World*. Or, better still, a book called *Jolly Roger* by Patrick Pringle, which has a very good chapter on Captain Kidd. Another excellent book on pirates, *On the Spanish Main*, is by John Masefield, who was once Poet Laureate of England.

You could also read *The Book of Buried Treasure* by Ralph D. Paine. He is the historian who found the French passes which might have saved the life of Captain Kidd.

If you want to hunt for treasure yourself, send 25 cents (no stamps) to the Library of Congress, Reference Department, Map Division, Washington, D.C. 20540, and ask for the booklet listing all the treasure maps in their collection. Then you can order the map for the area nearest you.

But be patient. And remember that the search is as much fun as the discovery—well, nearly as much fun. Robert Louis Stevenson, the author of *Treasure Island,* once heard that another author, Henry James, had never gone looking for buried treasure. "If he has never been on a quest for buried treasure," said Stevenson, "it can be demonstrated that he has never been a child."

A.B.C.W.
1970

Publisher's Note

After more than 300 years there has been an exciting discovery—the shipwreck of Captain Kidd's *Quedagh Merchant* has been found.

Its cannons were located by a snorkeler in 2007, in eight feet of water, about 70 feet off the rocky shore of Catalina Island in the Dominican Republic.

Archaeologists from Indiana University verified the ship was indeed the lost *Quedagh Merchant*. The cargo contents, a specific list of 10 tons of scrap metal, and the position of surplus anchors match Kidd's testimony. Lighter artifacts were likely to have been carried out to sea or washed up on the rocky shoreline.

The shipwreck and its maritime history are now preserved and protected as a Living Museum of the Seas curated by Indiana University and the Dominican government.

Divers visiting the shipwreck may view its rich history and observe the protected aquatic environment. A mooring buoy marks the spot; divers will find an underwater commemorative plaque and interpretive markers among the wreck. Divers are encouraged to take only pictures, leave only bubbles.

You can read more at https://underwaterscience.indiana.edu

If you'd like to pore over the treasure maps the author mentions in his note, it is much easier to access them now more than fifty years after this book was written.

Go to the Library of Congress website and search on "treasure maps" at https://www.loc.gov/maps

Happy hunting!

Index

Acts of Trade and Navigation, 9-10
Aden, Gulf of, 50, 52, 121
Admiralty Court, 3-4, 105, 108, 111
Adventure Galley (ship), 25-37, 80-81, 83, 90, 92, 107, 115, 122
Advice (ship), 41, 103-04
Anguilla, 82, 85
Antigua, 87
Antigua (ship), 12-13, 20, 24
Arabian Sea, 50, 52, 121

Babs Islands, 50-51, 83, 109
Barbados, 45, 86
Barlow, Edward, 55, 83
Barnacles, 47, 68, 76
Bellomont, Lord (Richard Coote), 13-16, 20, 23-24, 85, 92-101, 104-05, 111, 125
Bermuda, 40
Block Island, 118
Bolton, Henry, 87
Bombay, 66
Book of Buried Treasure, The (Paine), 120
Boston, 5, 8, 92, 94-95, 99-100, 103
Bradinham, Robert, 107-09, 117
British Museum, 117, 120
British Navy, 29-30, 44, 53, 67

Index

Cape Cod, 99
Cape Guardafui, 50
Cape of Good Hope, 17, 40, 43, 81-82, 103
Cape Town, 43
Carawar, 56
Cat-o'-nine-tails, used in Royal Navy, 67
Cochin coast, 77
Coniers (prosecuting attorney), 109
Coote, Richard (Lord Bellomont), 13-16, 20, 23-24, 85, 92-101, 104-05, 111, 125
Culliford, Robert, 12, 80-81, 108, 110, 122
Curacao, 87
Customs House, New York, 7, 35

Denmark, 85
Duchess (ship), 28, 30, 40

East India Company, 16-18, 26-27, 44, 53
East River, 7, 35
Emmot, James, 87-88, 90-95, 97-98, 123
England
  Tories in, 92, 104-05
  at war with France, 21, 31, 53
  Whigs in, 104-05
Every, Henry, 17-18, 45, 84, 117
Execution Dock, in London, 113

Fletcher, Benjamin, 11-13, 33
France, 51
  at war with England, 21, 31, 53

INDEX

French East India Company, 75
French passes
   concealed by Admiralty, 111, 117, 119
   Paine's discovery of, 117, 120

Gardiner, John, 97
Gardiner's Island, 95, 118, 124-25
Goa, 56-57
Good Hope, Cape of, 17, 40, 43, 81-82, 103
Great Mogul, 17-18, 117
Great Seal, King William's, 23, 28
Guardafui, Cape, 50
Gulf of Aden, 50, 52, 121
Gunsway (ship), 17

Harrison, Edmund, 27
Higüey River, 87, 123
Hispaniola, 87, 95, 123, 125-26
How, Captain, 61
Humphreys, Captain, 108

India, 11, 16-18, 44, 50, 56
Indian Ocean, 17, 43-44, 50, 117, 121

Johanna Island, 45

Keel-hauling, 68
Kidd (Rousby), Elizabeth, 8, 35-36, 88-89, 104, 117
Kidd, Sarah, 8, 31-32, 35-36, 88-89, 104, 117

INDEX

Kidd, William, 7-9, 11-16, 60-70, 72-77, 118, 121-26
  arrest of, 102, 123
  execution of, 116-17
  and French passes, concealment of, by Admiralty, 111, 117, 119
  map of voyage of, 38-39
  and Paine, 117, 120
  proclaimed a pirate, 83-84, 86, 89, 91
  sentenced to death, 3-4, 113
  and syndicate, 24, 32-33, 83, 90, 93-95, 98-99, 119
  and treasure, 95, 97, 124-26
  trial of, 3-4, 104-12, 119

Leeward Islands, 12
LeRoy (crewman), 74-75
Lewes, Delaware, 124
Livingston, Robert, 13-15, 18, 23-24
London, 3-4, 9, 13, 25, 92, 102
Long Island, 95
Long Island Sound, 87-88, 95, 118, 123-24
Lorentz, John, 86
Lovell, Salathiel, 106
Loyal Captain (ship), 61, 63, 65-66, 70

Madagascar, 43-44, 76-77, 79-80, 101, 110, 121-23
Madeira, 40, 46
Mahilla Island, 45-46, 48
Malabar Coast, 44, 56, 109
Malaria, 48

INDEX

Mecca, 50
Mocha fleets, 50-51, 53, 55-56, 83, 121
Money Island, 125
Moore, William, 62-63, 65-67, 69-73, 107, 109

Narragansett Bay, 97, 125
New York City, 4-10, 12-14, 32, 90-92, 100
Newgate prison, 3-4, 104, 113, 125
Newport, Rhode Island, 125
Nova Scotia, 118

Oort, Sarah. *See* Kidd, Sarah.
Owens, Abel, 107
Oyster Bay, 87-88, 95

Paine, Ralph D., 117, 120
Palmer, Joseph, 107-10, 117
Philadelphia, 5, 8
Piracy, 10-11, 16-17, 84, 120
Portugal, 56
Press gangs, 29, 32, 40
Privateers, 22-23
Public Records Office (London), 117, 120

Quedagh Merchant (ship), 79-87, 95, 110, 120, 123-24
Queensborough (ship), 86

Red Sea, 50-51
Rouparelle (ship), 75-76, 79-81, 83, 120-22, 124

INDEX

Rousby, Christopher, 117
Rousby (Kidd), Elizabeth, 8, 35-36, 88-89, 104, 117
Royal Navy, 29-30, 44, 53, 67

St. Anthony (ship), 87-88, 95, 97, 99, 123
St. Augustine settlement, 44
St. Martin Island, 12
St. Mary harbor, 80, 122
St. Thomas Island, 85-86
Sceptre (ship), 55, 83
Scurvy, 46
Silver Oar, of Admiralty Court, 4, 113
Smuggling, by colonists, 10
Stonington, Connecticut, 95
Stuart, Captain, 28, 30
Syndicate, and Kidd, 24, 32-33, 83, 90, 93-95, 98-99, 119

Telere (Toliara), 44
Teredo worms, 47, 76
Thames River, 104, 115, 117
Thimble Islands, 124-25
Tiger (ship), 41
Tilbury Fort, 117
Tory Party, 92, 104-05
Toliara (Telere), 44

Virginia, 5

Warren, Thomas, 41
West Indies, 8-12, 80, 82, 87, 108, 123
Whig Party, 104-05
William III, 13, 21, 23

About the Author

A. B. C. (Cal) Whipple made a lifelong hobby of the sea. As a youngster he used to explore Long Island Sound, and spent many vacations exploring the Bahamas and the West Indies, and ranged as far as the waters off England, Japan, and Hong Kong. It was while searching for possible treasure along Long Island Sound that Mr. Whipple realized young readers should be told the whole story of Captain Kidd.

Mr. Whipple's hobby resulted in several other maritime books, including *Yankee Whalers in the South Seas, Tall Ships and Great Captains, Famous Pirates of the New World,* and *Hero of Trafalgar: The Story of Lord Nelson.*

Born in Glen Falls, New York, Mr. Whipple was educated at the Loomis School in Connecticut, and at Yale and Harvard universities. He served as executive editor of Time-Life Books in New York and lived in Old Greenwich, Connecticut.

About the Illustrator

H. B. Vestal was the talented illustrator of numerous books for young readers. He studied art at the National Academy of Design and at the Pratt Institute. For three and a half years he served as a combat artist with the U.S. Coast Guard.

Mr. Vestal was a resident of New Jersey. Sailing as a hobby gave him a unique view in illustrating maritime subjects. Mr. Vestal has also illustrated the books *Walter Raleigh: Man of Two Worlds* and *The Voyages of Henry Hudson.*

www.ingramcontent.com/pod-product-compliance
Lightning Source LLC
Chambersburg PA
CBHW022326200825
31452CB00002B/10